MASTER SELF-CARE FOR WISE WOMEN

AN EMPOWERING 30-DAY PERSONAL DEVELOPMENT GUIDE TO ENHANCE HOLISTIC WELL-BEING, DEEPEN SELF-REFLECTION AND FIND YOUR PATHWAY TO INNER PEACE

NONIE ADAMS

CONTENTS

INTRODUCTION

Several years back, while serving in a senior leadership position abroad for a prominent organization, I found myself engulfed in the chaos of a demanding week. The convergence of tight deadlines and personal commitments had left me feeling swamped. With stress and anxiety levels rising, I paused to take a deep breath and decided to step outside my office for a quick walk. To my surprise, that simple act of self-care—just ten minutes of fresh air and movement—lifted my spirits and cleared my mind, allowing me to approach my tasks with renewed energy and perspective. This experience, small yet powerful, reminded me of something crucial: amidst life's relentless pace, taking time to care for ourselves is not just beneficial; it's necessary. It was an obvious sign of the power of self-care in our busy lives.

Self-care extends far beyond the occasional spa day or indulgent treat. It is a holistic approach that nurtures not just the body but also the mind and spirit. It integrates the science of well-being with practical, everyday actions and deep self-reflection to improve our overall health and happiness. Understanding how our brains respond to self-care practices can empower us to make choices that enhance our emotional, physical, and mental well-being.

"Master Self-Care for Wise Women" is not just another self-help book; it is a 30-day journey designed to introduce you to a balanced, neuroscience-backed approach to self-care. Each chapter offers concise, impactful strategies and applications that take no more than 10 minutes to implement, ensuring that even the busiest among us can find time to focus on ourselves. The holistic framework explored in this book addresses physical, emotional, mental, social, and spiritual self-care.

This guide is structured into six unique segments, each spanning five days and focusing on a different facet of women's self-care. These sections are rich with insightful information, inspiring narratives, and actionable steps for daily practice. You're invited to dedicate five days to deeply engage with each chapter, applying its teachings and reflecting through its activities to enrich your self-care journey. During this time, engage deeply with the journal prompts to foster thorough self-reflection. Once you feel ready and have gleaned the insights offered, you can advance to the next learning segment. In addition to these foundational chapters, two bonus sections await. These delve into sustaining your self-care journey—highlighting strategies for resetting and restarting – as well as exploring specialty topics like financial well-being and the vital role of resilience, creativity and legacy in self-care.

This book is for all women, irrespective of the stage of life or previous experience with self-care. The strategies and insights have been crafted to be inclusive and accessible, ensuring they resonate broadly and deeply.

Let's embark on this 30-day journey with an open mind and heart. Remember, self-care is a personal and evolving practice. This book is your first step towards finding what truly works for you in creating and sustaining a happier, healthier life.

Finally, as someone deeply committed to empowering women to lead more fulfilled lives, I am thrilled to share this guide with you. I hope that "Master Self-Care for Wise Women" will become a valuable tool in your journey, helping you reclaim your well-being and discover your pathway to inner peace. Let's begin this transformative exploration together, creating a life filled with joy, health, and serenity.

CHAPTER 1 (DAYS 1 – 5)
UNPACKING THE SCIENCE OF SELF-CARE

Have you ever felt like your brain was a browser with a hundred tabs open? Each tab represents a thought, a worry, a to-do list item screaming for attention. We've all been there, haven't we? In our fast-paced, hyper-connected lives, it's easy to feel overwhelmed. But what if I told you that you have the power to close those tabs one by one, to rewire your brain towards positivity and resilience through self-care? Intrigued? Let's dive into the fascinating world of neuroplasticity and discover how simple self-care practices can change your brain and life.

NEUROPLASTICITY AND SELF-CARE: REWIRING YOUR BRAIN FOR POSITIVITY

Understanding Neuroplasticity

Neuroplasticity might sound like a complex term, but it's really just your brain's ability to adapt and change as you learn and experience new things. Every time you acquire a new skill, indulge in a hobby, or even take a different route to work, you're tweaking your brain's wiring. This incredible adaptability isn't just about learning new things; it also plays a crucial role in how we can manage stress, develop resilience, and foster positivity through self-care.

Think about it this way: every habit, good or bad, forms a path in your brain. The more you walk down a particular path, the more defined it becomes. Negative habits carve pathways that can lead to anxiety and stress. Still, the good news is that positive habits do the opposite. They strengthen pathways that boost your well-being.

The Power of Positive Habits

Now, let's talk about these positive habits. Incorporating regular self-care practices into your routine isn't just pampering—it's a strategic move to sculpt your brain for positivity. When you engage in self-care—a morning meditation, a quick midday breathing exercise, or an evening gratitude journal—you're laying down neural pathways that fortify your resilience and uplift your mood. Just like a muscle grows stronger with regular exercise, your brain's positivity pathways become more robust with consistent self-care.

Mindfulness and Neuroplasticity

Mindfulness, in particular, is a superstar in enhancing brain plasticity. It's like taking your brain to the gym for a mental workout. Studies have shown that mindfulness meditation reduces stress and physically increases the grey matter in parts of the brain involved in emotion regulation and self-awareness. This means that mindfulness doesn't just help you feel better in the moment—it cultivates a more resilient and optimistic brain in the long term.

Overcoming Negative Thought Patterns

So, how can you use this knowledge to break free from cycles of negativity and self-doubt? It starts with awareness. Begin by identifying the negative thought patterns in your current mental routine. Each time you catch yourself slipping into old negative thinking habits, consciously choose a self-care activity that redirects your thoughts and creates a positive interaction in your brain.

For example, replace thoughts like "I can't handle this" with a few minutes of deep breathing or a walk outside. These actions aren't just symbolic—they physically alter your brain's response to stress and anxiety, making you more resilient.

Visualization Exercise: Rewiring Your Brain

Let's try a quick visualization exercise to put this into practice. Picture a network of roads in your mind where thoughts travel. See the roads filled with negative thoughts as dark and narrow paths, while positive thought highways are bright and wide. Whenever you practice a self-care activity, imagine it as construction work, widening the bright roads and adding beautiful landscapes. The more you work on it, the more inviting these roads become, making it easier for your thoughts to travel there naturally.

This chapter is just the beginning. As you explore and practice the self-care strategies discussed here, you'll feel better and fundamentally transform your brain for a happier, healthier life. Remember, each small step in self-care is a giant leap for your brain health. So, keep those sneakers—or should I say neural pathways—ready for action!

THE STRESS RESPONSE: MANAGING CORTISOL THROUGH MINDFUL PRACTICES

Let's talk about stress. Not your garden-variety, missed-the-bus stress, but the kind that makes you wolf down a chocolate bar or snap at the cat. When life throws its curveballs, our bodies react by pumping cortisol, commonly known as the "stress hormone." This ancient biological response, designed to help our ancestors flee from lions and tigers, can wreak havoc on our modern bodies when triggered too frequently. Elevated cortisol levels can lead to many unwelcome issues like weight gain, sleep disturbances, and a weakened immune system. It's like your body's not-so-helpful way of saying, "Hey, I'm trying to save you here," while simultaneously flooding your engine.

Now, enter Mindfulness-Based Stress Reduction (MBSR). Developed in the late 1970s by Dr Jon Kabat-Zinn, MBSR is a structured program that uses mindfulness meditation to address the unconscious thoughts, feelings, and behaviours thought to increase stress and undermine your health. Imagine if you could train your brain to respond to stress with a calm observation rather than a flurry of panic. MBSR does just that—it teaches you to handle stress with mindfulness, thereby reducing your body's cortisol production. Think of it as training your brain to put that chocolate bar down and step away slowly. It's about observing the stressors without letting them take the wheel.

Practising MBSR can start with something as simple and as fundamental as breathing. Yes, breathing! Not the shallow, barely-there breaths you take when you're typing furiously at your computer, but deep, soul-soothing breaths. Let's try this together: close your eyes (after you read this, of course), take a slow breath in through your nose, let your chest and belly expand fully, hold it for a second, and exhale slowly through your mouth. Do this a few times. Feel better? You've just engaged in a powerful, immediate form of stress reduction. These breathing exercises are portable, require zero equipment, and can be done in any stressful scenario—from a packed subway car to a contentious work meeting.

But how do we make this a regular part of our lives and not just a one-off trick for calming down during a stressful email exchange? This is where creating a personalized stress-management plan comes into play. It's about integrating mindful practices into your daily routine, so they become as habitual as brushing your teeth. Begin by identifying the times of day or the situations where stress peaks. Is it during the morning rush, before a weekly meeting, or when managing finances? Allocate a few minutes before or during these times for a mindfulness practice. It could be a series of deep breaths, a full 10-minute meditation, or even a few moments of mindful walking. The key is consistency. Much like watering a plant, regular care makes your mindfulness practice thrive.

Incorporating MBSR and other mindful practices into your daily routine helps manage cortisol levels and, by extension, reduces stress's physical and psychological impacts. By training your brain to respond differently to stress, you actively change its wiring, improving health and increased well-being. It's a transformation that begins with a single breath and evolves into a more serene approach to life's inevitable challenges. So the next time you reach for that chocolate bar in a moment of stress, remember that a deep breath can be just as sweet.

THE ROLE OF DOPAMINE IN HABIT FORMATION: LEVERAGING HAPPINESS

Dopamine often gets a bad rap as the "feel-good" chemical that keeps you reaching for another piece of chocolate or one more episode on a binge-watch. But there's more to this neurotransmitter than the instant gratification tag it's been saddled with. Dopamine is essentially your brain's reward system announcer; it plays a critical role in cultivating habits, particularly those linked to our happiness and well-being. Understanding how dopamine functions can unlock the secret to forming and maintaining healthy self-care habits that stick.

Let's break it down: imagine you're sipping your favourite coffee or tea, feeling the warmth as it travels down, or the smell of rain-soaked earth—these little pleasures trigger dopamine release. This release signals to your brain, "Hey, this feels good. Let's do it again." That's dopamine working as a reward signal. It's crucial for habit formation because it helps reinforce the activities that make us feel good, encouraging us to repeat them. Now, think about applying this to self-care. When you take a short walk during a break or meditate for a few minutes in the morning, and it feels rejuvenating, dopamine cheers you on from the sidelines, whispering, "Yes, keep this up!"

Harnessing this dopamine effect can be particularly potent when building self-care habits. By understanding that this chemical makes our brains pay attention to rewards, you can manipulate your habits to make self-care as addictive (in a healthy way) as that morning cup of coffee. For instance, setting up a reward system for yourself can amplify this effect. After a week of sticking to your meditation routine, you treat yourself to a spa day or a new book. This reward boosts your brain's dopamine levels and motivates you to stick to the self-care regimen.

Speaking of sticking to regimens, let's talk about the "Small Wins Strategy." The journey of a thousand miles begins with a single step, right? Well, building a robust self-care habit starts with small, achievable goals. These goals are your small wins. When you set a massive goal, it's easy to get overwhelmed and give up when immediate results aren't visible. But small goals? They're doable. Each time you achieve one, dopamine does its thing, and you feel a surge of satisfaction. This feeling then fuels your motivation to tackle the next goal. It's a beautiful cycle. For example, instead of aiming to meditate for an hour each day, start with five minutes. Achieve that for a week, then increase it by another five minutes. Small, yes, but each step is a win, and each win is a dopamine-rich step towards a lasting habit.

However, balancing this dopamine-driven pursuit of happiness with productivity is crucial. It's easy to skew towards activities that offer immediate dopamine hits but aren't necessarily beneficial in the long run (hello, social media scrolling). To ensure that your dopamine-driven habits contribute positively to your well-being, focus on integrating activities that offer long-term rewards into your routine. For instance, replace that mid-afternoon social media check with a quick walk or a few stretches. Both activities increase dopamine and improve your health and productivity.

Incorporating these strategies effectively means you are not just at the mercy of your brain's wiring; you are taking the reins and steering them towards habits that foster long-term well-being. Each small, dopamine-rich step builds a path to a healthier, happier you, where self-care becomes a part of your daily life, as natural and necessary as breathing.

OXYTOCIN AND CONNECTION: THE SCIENCE OF SOCIAL BONDS

Oxytocin Explained

Often dubbed the "love hormone," oxytocin is your brain's way of enhancing social connections, trust, and bonding. This remarkable little hormone plays a crucial role in the human ability to form relationships, from romantic partnerships to friendships and even the bond between mother and child. When oxytocin levels are high, we feel happier, more connected, and less anxious. It's like nature's built-in anti-anxiety medication, but instead of swallowing a pill, you get a hug, have a heartfelt conversation, or share a laugh with friends. The science behind oxytocin is fascinating—it shows us that our bodies are designed to connect with others and that doing so can improve our mental health and emotional resilience.

Now, you might wonder how a simple hormone can profoundly impact our interactions with others. When oxytocin is released in response to social interactions, it affects the amygdala, the area of the brain involved in emotional processing and fear response. By reducing the activity in the amygdala, oxytocin helps us to feel less stressed and more serene. It's akin to lowering the volume of your stress and turning up the dial on your contentment. This biochemical shift not only makes us feel good at the moment but also reinforces the behaviours that led to the release of oxytocin, making us more likely to seek out positive social interactions in the future.

Social Self-Care

Given the powerful effects of oxytocin, social self-care is a potent strategy for enhancing our well-being. Social self-care involves making time for meaningful interactions with others, which can significantly boost your mood and provide support through life's ups and downs. It's about recognizing that movie dates, phone calls and messages to old friends, and family dinners aren't just fun but fundamental to our well-being. Each of these interactions releases oxytocin, which, in turn, reduces stress and fosters a sense of connectedness.

Imagine sitting down to a cup of tea, or a glass of wine, with a friend, sharing stories, and catching up on each other's lives. Such simple acts of connection do more than pass the time; they knit the fabric of our social support network tighter. This network acts as a buffer against the stresses of life, making us feel supported and understood. It's about creating a community of care, where laughter and empathy are abundant, and isolation and stress are kept at bay.

Building Support Networks

Building and maintaining a robust support network is one of the most valuable investments you can make in your emotional well-being. Start by reaching out to friends and family regularly, not just when feeling down. Consistency is key. It's like watering a garden; it thrives with regular care. Additionally, consider joining clubs or groups that align with your interests. Whether it's a book club, a yoga class, or a gardening group, these settings offer unique opportunities to meet new people who share your passions, further expanding your support network.

Moreover, please don't underestimate the power of giving support as well as receiving it. Helping others can bolster your sense of purpose and increase your own feelings of well-being. It's a beautiful cycle:

- Your support helps them.
- Their gratitude and connection boost your mood.
- Everyone's oxytocin levels increase, making the whole group happier and more connected.

The Role of Physical Touch

Physical touch is another potent oxytocin releaser. A hug, a pat on the back, or even a friendly handshake can increase your oxytocin levels and reduce stress. In relationships, daily acts of physical affection, such as cuddling, holding hands, or a reassuring touch, are not only expressions of love but crucial for maintaining a strong, emotional connection and a sense of intimacy. This doesn't mean you need to go around hugging everyone in sight, but it does mean that incorporating affectionate touch into your daily interactions can profoundly benefit your emotional and physical health.

Consider, for example, the simple act of hugging a friend when you meet them. This brief, warm embrace can significantly boost your mood and theirs, reinforcing your mutual bond and providing a moment of comfort and connection. In a world that often prioritizes digital communication over face-to-face interactions, remembering the power of touch is more important than ever. These tangible expressions of care and connection fortify our relationships and enrich our lives.

In sum, understanding and leveraging the power of oxytocin through social self-care, nurturing your support networks, and embracing the role of physical touch are not just strategies for building happier, healthier lives; they're foundational practices that enable us to connect deeply with others, enhancing our own emotional well-being and that of those around us. As we continue to explore the multifaceted world of self-care, remember that each interaction, each touch, and each connection plays a crucial role in weaving the rich tapestry of our social and emotional lives.

NUTRITION'S IMPACT ON MENTAL HEALTH: EATING FOR HAPPINESS

Let's talk about food, but not just any food—food that feeds your brain and nourishes your soul. It's fascinating how the adage "you are what you eat" holds more truth than we ever gave it credit for, especially when it comes to mental health. Have you ever considered that your gut could be your second brain? Well, science says it is. This little powerhouse, the gut-brain axis, is a communication network that links your gut and brain biologically and biochemically. Factors in your gut can influence your brain, and conversely, your brain can influence gut behaviours. This connection means your food can directly affect your brain's structure and functionality, ultimately impacting your mood and mental health.

Imagine your gastrointestinal tract as a busy highway system where food is the traffic, and the neurotransmitters are the traffic signals. When the traffic flows smoothly, and the signals work correctly, your mood tends to be more balanced and your mind clearer. This is because about 95% of serotonin, the critical hormone that stabilizes our mood, feelings of well-being, and happiness, is produced in your gastrointestinal tract. So, maintaining a healthy gut isn't just about avoiding stomach aches; it's about fostering a well-balanced mind. Foods rich in probiotics like yogurt, kefir, and fermented vegetables can help enhance this gut-brain communication, promoting a happier and healthier you.

Now, let's delve into the specific nutrients that play starring roles in the saga of your brain health. Omega-3 fatty acids, for example, are like the superheroes of the nutritional world. Found abundantly in fish like salmon and sardines, they help build and repair brain cells. Omega-3s are integral to the structure of brain cells, particularly the cell membranes. They are known to enhance the function of neurotransmitters, which means better mood control and less brain fog. Then there's magnesium, found in leafy greens and nuts, which acts like a bouncer at a club, regulating neurotransmitters and calming the nervous system, thus helping you feel more relaxed and less frazzled. And we can't forget about antioxidants—those excellent compounds that fight off the oxidative stress that ages your brain. You can load up on these brain protectors by eating colourful fruits and vegetables like blueberries, spinach, and beets.

Finally, let's discuss integrating these insights into practical strategies for nutritional well-being. It starts with a kitchen makeover—out with the processed, sugar-laden foods that spike your blood sugar and mood, and in with the whole, unprocessed foods that nourish and sustain you. Plan your meals around your mental health needs; for instance, incorporate more fermented foods and fibre if you're feeling down, as these can boost gut health and mood. Always hydrate—sometimes, dehydration disguises itself as a bad mood. Remember, implementing these changes is not about striving for perfection but making better choices one meal at a time. It's about creating a diet that feeds not just your body but also your brain.

As you continue to explore the profound impact of nutrition on your mental health, keep in mind that every bite you take can be a step toward a happier, healthier mind. Like a well-loved recipe, your diet can always be adjusted and improved. So, keep experimenting, keep learning, and let your meals be a source of joy and mental clarity. After all, eating for happiness is about finding the right ingredients to create a delicious and fulfilling life.

Reflection Section – Nourishing Your Happiness

"Happiness is not a goal; it's a byproduct."

ELEANOR ROOSEVELT

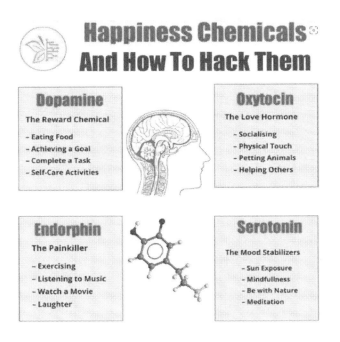

As we have just explored, our sense of happiness emerges not as a direct aim but as a natural consequence of our body's intricate physiological mechanisms, notably by releasing certain neurotransmitters and hormones. This section's accompanying infographic (Happiness hormones - MEDizzy) concisely overviews our brain's, 'happiness hormones.' It underscores the importance of harmonizing these 'happiness chemicals' with a holistic lifestyle approach, emphasizing the necessity of consistent, restorative sleep, regular physical activity, balanced nutrition, healthy self-care habits and choices and enriching social engagements.

Pause for a moment of reflection and jot down your thoughts in a journal:

- Identify the daily practices you currently employ to elevate your neurotransmitters and overall well-being. Which of these practices do you find most effective?

To further enhance your holistic well-being through simple, yet effective actions, consider the following strategies tailored to boost various neurotransmitters in your brain:

For **Dopamine**, which fuels our drive and motivation, set achievable goals, establish self-care routines, and embrace the learning of new skills to stimulate this neurotransmitter's production.

To increase **Serotonin**, known as the mood stabilizer, seek out more sunlight by spending time outdoors, immerse yourself in nature walks, and reflect through the process of journaling. These activities can elevate your serotonin levels, leading to a more balanced emotional state.

Encouraging the release of **Oxytocin**, the love hormone, can be as simple as incorporating more physical touch, committing random acts of kindness, and enjoying moments with pets. These interactions enhance feelings of connection and love.

Lastly, to boost **Endorphins**, the body's natural painkillers, engage in regular exercise, look for opportunities to laugh, and delve into creative pursuits, such as drawing, playing an instrument and cooking. These activities not only improve your physical health but also contribute to a sense of happiness and well-being.

In your journal, identify which strategies resonate with you the most. Dedicate yourself to experimenting with some new practices over the coming five days. Observe and record any shifts in your mood, energy levels, or overall well-being.

A h, change. It's that thing we all say we want until it shows up, demanding we put down the chocolate and pick up a kale smoothie. But before you run for the hills (or the fridge), let's talk about setting the foundation for change that sticks, especially when it comes to self-care. It all starts with understanding and aligning your personal values. Think of your values as your personal North Star—they guide you, keep you on track, and ensure your self-care journey feels right and rings true to who you are.

IDENTIFYING PERSONAL VALUES AND HOW THEY INFLUENCE SELF-CARE

Understanding Your Core Values

Imagine you're a detective in a film noir, trench coat and all, sifting through the clues of your life to uncover your core values. What drives you? What are the non-negotiable elements that define your actions and decisions? Identifying these core values isn't just about introspection; it's an exercise in honesty. It's peeling back the layers of "shoulds" and "musts" imposed by society, family, or that very persuasive internet influencer to reveal what truly matters to you—perhaps freedom, compassion, stability, or creativity.

One effective method to unearth these values is to think about times when you felt most fulfilled or pleased with your decisions. What were the common elements of these situations? Perhaps you felt a sense of accomplishment when you helped a friend in need, highlighting 'compassion' as a core value. Or maybe you felt immense satisfaction after completing a challenging project at work, underscoring 'achievement' as a guiding principle. Recognizing these patterns helps you pinpoint the values that are the bedrock of your being.

Values and Self-Care Alignment

Now, why is aligning your self-care practices with these values so crucial? Simply put, when your self-care activities echo your values, they feel less like a chore and more like a natural part of your life. For instance, if one of your core values is 'connection,' scheduling regular meet-ups with friends can be a form of self-care. Similarly, if 'learning' tops your list, attending workshops or reading books might be your go-to self-care strategy. By aligning your self-care with your values, each action becomes more impactful and fulfilling, deeply rooting these practices in your daily routine.

Values-Based Goal Setting

Setting goals based on your values isn't just about what you aim to achieve; it's about how you reach these milestones. Let's say your core value is 'integrity.' Your self-care goals might then focus on activities that enhance your self-respect and authenticity, perhaps through yoga, meditation, or journaling. These goals carry a weight that resonates with your deeper self, making them more compelling and easier to commit to. They're not just items on a to-do list but stepping stones to a more authentic you.

Navigating Life Changes

Life, the ever-dynamic journey, throws curveballs that can sometimes send our well-laid plans for self-care into a tailspin. Here's where your values come in handy again. Consider them your compass in the stormy seas of change. Whether it's a career shift, a move to a new city, or any other significant life transition, your values can guide your decisions and help maintain a focus on self-care. They remind you of what's important, ensuring your self-care practices adapt to support these priorities rather than getting lost in the shuffle.

SETTING REALISTIC SELF-CARE GOALS: THE SMART METHOD

When it comes to self-care, setting goals can sometimes feel like deciding to clean out that one junk drawer in your kitchen — you know it needs doing, but where do you even start? That's where the SMART method swoops in, not just with a cape but with a plan. SMART stands for Specific, Measurable, Achievable/Attractive, Relevant, and Time-bound. It's a tried-and-true formula that breaks down the lofty ideal of "self-care" into tangible, achievable goals. Let's unpack this together, shall we?

Goal Setting Principles: Introduction to the SMART Method

Think of the SMART method as your self-care blueprint. To start, your goals need to be **Specific**. Vague goals are like trying to catch fog — frustrating and futile. Instead of saying, "I want to relax more," specify what relaxation looks like for you. Is it reading, gardening, or perhaps meditating? Next, ensure your goals are **Measurable**. Attach numbers to them! Decide how many pages you'll read or how many minutes you'll meditate each day. This measurability lets you see your progress rather than guessing if you're getting closer to your goal.

The **Achievable** aspect is about setting goals that are challenging yet within reach. If you haven't jogged in years, setting a goal to run a marathon in a month is like setting yourself up for a date with disappointment. Start with smaller, achievable goals, like jogging twice weekly, and gradually increase your target. The A in the SMART acronym can also mean **Attractive**. Suppose the goal is not something that you find exciting and inspiring. In that case, you are unlikely to be motivated to achieve it. **Relevance** is crucial because your goals must align with your life's current priorities and overall well-being. There's no point in forcing yourself to wake up at 5 AM for yoga if you're a night owl and it makes you miserable. Lastly, **Time-bound** means setting a deadline. Without a specific timeframe, there's no sense of urgency, and your goal might get perpetually postponed to 'someday.'

Breaking Down Big Goals: How to break larger self-care objectives into manageable, actionable steps

We often look at our ultimate goal, which looms over us like a daunting and seemingly impossible mountain. The trick is to break it down into smaller, manageable hills that you can conquer step by step. Let's say your goal is to reduce stress through meditation. Instead of a fluffy aim of "meditate more," start with "meditate for five minutes every morning for two weeks." Once that becomes a habit, increase the duration or add a second session in the evening. Each small victory gets you closer to your larger goal and boosts your confidence and motivation.

Monitoring Progress: Techniques for tracking your self-care journey and adjusting goals as needed

Tracking progress can be the make-or-break factor in achieving your self-care goals. It's not just about ticking off boxes; it's a way to visualize your journey, celebrate your progress, and adjust your sails when needed. You can use a journal, an app, or even a simple spreadsheet. The key is consistency and honesty in your tracking. Every week, take a moment to review your progress. Are you consistently meeting your goals? Great! Maybe it's time to stretch them a bit further. Finding it challenging to meet your goals? No problem. Consider what's holding you back and adjust your goals to be more achievable. This adaptability keeps your self-care journey realistic and flexible.

Celebrating Successes: The importance of recognizing and celebrating achievements to maintain motivation

Every milestone deserves a celebration. Whether sticking to your meditation schedule for a month or tackling that kitchen drawer (you know the one), take time to celebrate these wins. Celebration can be a powerful motivator, reinforcing your commitment to self-care. How you celebrate is up to you — it might be a small treat, a day out, or simply an hour spent doing something you love. These celebrations are not just rewards; they are affirmations of your progress, reminders that you can meet the goals you set for yourself, no matter how small they seem.

As you weave the SMART method into your self-care strategy, remember that the goal isn't perfection but progress. It's about making self-care a consistent and enjoyable part of your life, one SMART goal at a time.

THE IMPORTANCE OF ROUTINE IN BUILDING SELF-CARE HABITS

Let's face it, the word "routine" might bring to mind a life of monotonous repetition, like brushing your teeth or doing the dishes. But when it comes to self-care, establishing a routine could be the secret sauce that turns "I should do this" into "I got this." Imagine your daily routine as a cozy blanket; it's familiar, comforting, and supportive. Just as a blanket provides warmth, a well-crafted routine offers a structure that warms up your motivation and wraps your day in predictability, making the chaos a bit more manageable.

Routine's Role in Habit Formation

Think of your brain as a creature of habit. It loves patterns and predictability. When you establish a routine, you're essentially training your brain to expect and embrace certain activities at certain times. This predictability reduces the mental load of deciding what to do and when, freeing up cognitive resources for other tasks. For instance, if you decide that every morning starts with a ten-minute meditation session, your brain begins to anticipate this activity as a regular start to the day. Over time, this anticipation helps cement meditation as a habit, making it more automatic and less of a battle to find the time or motivation. It's like setting a coffee pot to brew at the same time each morning; eventually, it's the natural start to your day, and everything feels off without it.

Crafting a Personalized Self-Care Routine

Creating a self-care routine that sticks isn't about copying someone else's schedule; it's about designing a routine that fits your lifestyle and resonates with your needs. Start by assessing the best times in your day for undisturbed self-care. Maybe you're an early bird who thrives by having time alone in the morning, or perhaps you're a night owl whose creativity sparks after sunset. Use these natural tendencies to your advantage. Next, consider the types of activities that genuinely help you recharge. If a 20-minute workout leaves you energized, slot it in. If reading calms your mind, make time for it. The key is to mix necessity with enjoyment; your routine should include elements you need to do for your well-being, sprinkled with things you love doing. This blend ensures your routine is beneficial and enjoyable, increasing the likelihood of sticking with it.

The Power of Consistency

Here's where the magic happens. Consistency in your routine transforms occasional self-care into a dependable source of rejuvenation. The regularity signals to your mind and body, "Hey, it's time to slow down and take care of ourselves." This signal helps ease the transition into self-care activities, making them feel as natural and essential as eating or sleeping. Consistent practice also builds momentum. Each day you stick to your routine reinforces your commitment and boosts your confidence in managing your well-being. It's like building a bridge; each plank is crucial, and although it takes time and effort, the result is a stable path to the other side—better health and happiness.

Adjusting Routines for Growth

Just because routines are about consistency doesn't mean they're set in stone. Your self-care needs will likely shift as you grow and your life changes. Regularly assess your routine to ensure it still serves your highest good. Are you feeling bored? Maybe it's time to spice things up with a new activity. Have your circumstances changed? Adjust your routine to align with your current reality. Maybe you've started a new job and must shift your yoga sessions from morning to evening. These tweaks aren't signs of failure; they prove that you're in tune with yourself and committed to maintaining self-care as a dynamic part of your life. Remember, the goal of a routine is to support you consistently, not constrain you rigidly.

As you craft and refine your self-care routine, think of it as sculpting a masterpiece. It starts as a rough block of marble, but with each chisel strike, or in this case, each day you engage in your routine, you shape it into a form that beautifully enhances your life. This ongoing process of carving out time, adjusting activities, and striving for consistency isn't just about building habits; it's about crafting a lifestyle that continuously fuels and fulfils you. So, grab that chisel, and let's sculpt a routine that resonates with your unique rhythm and needs.

OVERCOMING OBSTACLES: TIME MANAGEMENT STRATEGIES FOR BUSY WOMEN

Ah, time management – that elusive juggling act that every woman tries to master while balancing a coffee in one hand and her aspirations in the other. It's easy to let the day slip through your fingers, pulled in a million directions by tasks that, upon reflection, might not even be essential. So, let's tackle this head-on, shall we? Starting with those sneaky little gremlins I call 'time thieves'. These are the activities that gobble up your precious minutes without contributing anything meaningful to your life. It could be mindlessly scrolling through social media, overcommitting to favours, or attending unnecessary meetings that could have been emailed (oh, how we love those!).

Identifying these time thieves is your first step. For a week, play the role of a time detective. Keep a log of your daily activities and how long each one takes. Be brutally honest with yourself. How much time are you spending on things that don't align with your personal or professional goals? You might discover that an hour of social media can be trimmed down to 15 minutes or that doing laundry daily can be consolidated to twice a week. This isn't about stripping down your day to a robotic schedule; it's about making room for the things that truly matter – like your self-care.

Next up, let's talk about prioritization. This is the art of knowing what needs your attention first and what can wait. It's about aligning your daily activities with broader life goals and values. Start by categorizing your tasks into 'must-dos', 'should-dos', and 'nice-to-dos'. Your self-care activities? They go into the 'must-dos'. Yes, you heard that right. Prioritizing self-care is not about selfishness; it's about ensuring you're at your best, which allows you to be more present for others and your work. Each morning or the night before, list your top three self-care must-dos and slot them into your schedule as non-negotiable appointments. This might mean waking up 30 minutes earlier to meditate, taking a midday walk, or reading before bed. The key is commitment, treating these self-care appointments with the same seriousness as a work meeting.

Now, let's spice up your time management with a technique called 'time blocking'. This method involves dedicating specific blocks of time to similar tasks or single tasks, minimizing the transition time between different types of work and reducing task-switching fatigue. Create blocks of time in your schedule for work, self-care, family, and leisure. During each block, focus solely on tasks from that category. For instance, you might block an early morning period for exercise, a late morning slot for deep-focus work tasks, and an evening window for family time. This method helps you manage your day efficiently and ensures that self-care becomes a structured part of your routine, not something that's squeezed into leftover gaps.

Handling unexpected disruptions is like playing a game of Tetris with your schedule—sometimes, things just don't fit neatly. Flexibility and a solid backup plan are key to managing these disruptions. Start by identifying parts of your routine that are most vulnerable to interruptions. Have a plan B for these times. If you usually jog in the park but it's raining, have a quick indoor workout routine as a backup. If a last-minute work emergency eats into your reading time, shift it to right before bed. Communicate your boundaries clearly with colleagues, friends, and family so they know when you are unavailable. And most importantly, maintain a buffer in your schedule—a little free time not allocated to any specific tasks. This buffer cushions unexpected events, ensuring they don't completely throw off your day.

Managing time, particularly for self-care, in today's fast-paced world is not about doing more; it's about doing what's meaningful. It's about recognizing that while you can't control time, you can control your actions. By becoming a masterful time manager, you ensure that self-care is not left to the whims of a chaotic schedule but is a deliberate and cherished part of your life. So, as you continue to navigate your busy days, remember that each minute is a new opportunity to prioritize, organize, and harmonize your life in a way that leaves room for what you need to do and what you love to do.

THE ART OF SAYING NO: BOUNDARY SETTING FOR SELF-PRESERVATION

Let's face it, saying "no" can sometimes feel as daunting as singing a solo at karaoke night—sweaty palms, shaky legs, etc. But here's the thing—mastering the art of saying no is not just about guarding your time; it's about respecting your energy, your priorities, and, ultimately, your well-being. Think of boundaries as your personal security system; they keep the good things in and the bad things out. They help you navigate personal and professional waters without feeling you're drowning in other people's expectations. So, let's get you comfortable setting boundaries that rock solid, shall we?

The Importance of Boundaries

Imagine a garden. Without a fence, anyone can trample through, picking your flowers and leaving footprints in their wake. But with a sturdy fence, your garden thrives, protected from unwanted intrusions. Your energy and peace of mind are like that garden, needing protection to flourish. Setting boundaries is not about shutting people out; it's about allowing yourself to thrive. It's allowing yourself to prioritize your needs, manage your energy, and engage in activities that replenish rather than drain you. When you set clear boundaries, you communicate to others what's acceptable and what's not, preserving your well-being and fostering healthier interactions with those around you.

Practical Ways to Say No

Saying no might be simple in theory, but it's an art in practice. The key is to be direct yet diplomatic. Instead of a blunt "no," which can come off as harsh or uncooperative, try cushioning it with appreciation and a clear rationale. For instance, if a friend invites you to a social gathering on a day you've set aside for self-care, respond with, "I appreciate you thinking of me, but I need to keep this time to recharge. Can we find another time to catch up?" This approach acknowledges the request, validates your refusal, and opens the door for alternative solutions, making the "no" easier to digest.

Another technique is to delay your response instead of giving an immediate answer. Use phrases like, "Let me check my schedule and get back to you." This gives you time to evaluate the request against your priorities and prepare a reasoned response. Remember, whenever you say yes to something that doesn't align with your well-being, you're potentially saying no to something that does. So, make your yeses count and keep your nos clear and kind.

The Impact of Boundaries on Relationships

You might worry that setting boundaries will push people away, but what it actually does is clarify your relationships. Communicating your limits, you help prevent resentment and misunderstandings that can strain relationships. Boundaries create a clear framework within which healthy relationships can thrive. They help people understand how to interact with you in a way that respects both parties' needs and preferences. For instance, by telling your family that Sunday mornings are your quiet time, you set an expectation that you are not available for calls or visits during those hours, which can help prevent feelings of frustration on both sides. Far from harming your relationships, well-communicated boundaries can deepen them, building mutual respect and understanding.

Self-Care and Professional Boundaries

The workplace can often feel like a boundary-free zone, where requests and demands flood your desk unabated. Setting professional boundaries is crucial to maintaining not only your sanity but also your effectiveness at work. Start by being clear about your work hours. If you're done at 6 PM, be consistent about logging off and communicate this to your colleagues. If you're inundated with tasks, learn to delegate or discuss priorities with your supervisor. A simple, "Given my current workload, which of these projects would you like me to prioritize?" can help set the right expectations and prevent burnout.

Moreover, be mindful of not letting work bleed into your personal life. This might mean turning off email notifications after hours or setting a no-call rule during dinner. Remember, being always available doesn't make you more valuable; it makes you more vulnerable to stress and burnout. Setting these boundaries protects your time and signals to others that you respect and manage your time well, which can increase their respect for you.

As you navigate the delicate art of setting boundaries, remember it's a process. It takes practice, and yes, sometimes you'll falter. But each attempt strengthens your boundary-setting muscles, making it easier each time. So, go ahead and set those boundaries with confidence. Your well-being isn't just your priority; it's your right. And who knows? You might just inspire others to start setting their own boundaries, too. Now, wouldn't that be something?

CULTIVATING SELF-COMPASSION: MOVING BEYOND SELF-JUDGMENT

Let's talk about self-compassion, a superpower that doesn't get nearly enough credit. It's the gentle yet radically powerful art of being as kind to yourself as you would be to a dear friend in distress. Often, we're our own toughest critics, and let's be honest, that inner critic can be downright nasty. It's time to learn how to turn down its volume and tune into a kinder, more supportive voice.

Defining Self-Compassion

Self-compassion involves treating yourself with the same kindness, concern, and support you'd offer someone you care about deeply. Dr Kristin Neff, a leading expert in this field, breaks it down into three components:

- Self-kindness (being warm towards yourself when you fail or feel inadequate).
- Common humanity (recognizing that suffering and personal failure are part of the shared human experience).
- Mindfulness (holding your thoughts and emotions in balanced awareness).

Embracing these aspects can transform how you relate to yourself, especially when you stumble or face challenges.

Practices to Cultivate Self-Compassion

Now, how do we cultivate this wonderful quality? Start with self-kindness. Next time you flub up or let someone down, instead of beating yourself up, try soothing yourself. Place your hand over your heart, feel its rhythm, and offer yourself some comforting words. It might feel awkward at first, but there's science behind this: physical gestures of warmth can activate the release of oxytocin, the same hormone released when you get a hug.

Mindfulness is another key player in the self-compassion league. It allows you to observe your thoughts and feelings with openness and curiosity without over-identifying with them. You can practice this by simply noticing your breath or stepping back and observing your thoughts as if they were clouds passing in the sky, neither clinging to them nor pushing them away. This helps create a space between you and your reactions, providing room for a more compassionate response.

Finally, to foster a sense of common humanity, remind yourself that you're not alone in your struggles. Everyone messes up, everyone suffers, and everyone feels inadequate at times. This perspective can be incredibly liberating; it allows you to let go of that harsh, judgmental voice that says you're the only one struggling.

Self-Compassion in Difficult Times

Self-compassion becomes particularly crucial during tough times. When you're going through a rough patch, ramp up your self-compassion practices. You might write a letter to yourself from the perspective of a compassionate friend or simply allow yourself to grieve without self-judgment. This approach doesn't just alleviate pain; it builds resilience, enabling you to recover more quickly and emerge stronger.

Self-compassion isn't about self-indulgence or lowering your standards. It's about acknowledging your humanity—your imperfections included—and treating yourself with the same dignity and understanding you'd offer others. It's a practice, a commitment, and yes, sometimes a challenge, but it's worth every moment. By cultivating self-compassion, you're enhancing your relationship with yourself and enriching how you interact with the world. It's a profound transformation that begins with a simple shift in how you treat yourself.

As we wrap up this chapter on laying the groundwork for change, remember that these practices aren't just tasks to check off; they're steps toward a more intentional, compassionate way of living. Whether aligning your goals with your values, setting realistic targets, establishing nurturing routines, managing your time wisely, setting healthy boundaries, or fostering self-compassion, each aspect is about crafting a life that honours and supports your true self. As we move forward, carry these tools with you, ready to face the challenges and embrace the joys of your self-care path. Next, we will explore how these foundational practices can enhance your physical well-being, bringing us into deeper harmony with our bodies.

 Reflection Section – Valuing Your Values

"When your values are clear to you, making decisions becomes easier."

ROY E DISNEY

Values help us determine what is important and meaningful to us, and what isn't. This ensures we live a life that holds purpose for us, enhancing and generating positive emotions and increased levels of well-being. Alan Kovitz says, *"Our values are non-negotiable and determine how we show up in the world. When we live our values, we assign meaning to our lives and our happiness manifests."*, (*A Book of Values*).

Individuals who align their daily lives with their core values experience enhanced well-being. To continue this journey of discovery, consider the following strategies for uncovering your values:

1. Take an online quiz such as the Personal Values Assessment
2. Purchase a set of Values Cards
3. Select your top 5-10 values from a list of values available on the internet

Take a moment now to jot down your top five values. Reflect on how these have shaped your life decisions and consider how they can guide your self-care practices. This reflection is not just an exercise; it's a commitment to making self-care a true reflection of who you are.

Consider using these prompts to guide you towards a deeper understanding of your personal values through structured reflection:

- **Defining moment**: write about a time when you felt genuinely proud of a decision you made/ What values were you upholding?
- **Challenging situations**: Describe a situation where you faced a moral dilemma. What values were in conflict, and how did you resolve it?
- **Inspirations**: Who are the people who you most admire, and what values do they embody that you aspire to or admire greatly?
- **Future legacy**: Imagine it's many years in the future; what would you want to be remembered for? How do these elements reflect your values?
- **Daily actions**: What are actions you regularly take that reflect your core values? Are there actions you wish to change or adopt to better align with your values?

As we continue exploring the foundations of self-care, remember that aligning your practices with your values isn't about adding more to your plate; it's about ensuring that every bite nourishes you deeply, resonating with the core of your being. This alignment is the secret sauce that makes the pursuit of well-being sustainable and deeply satisfying. So, keep those values close—they're the keys to unlocking a personalized and profoundly effective self-care regimen.

CHAPTER 3 (DAYS 11 – 15)
PHYSICAL WELL-BEING AS SELF-CARE

W hen caring for our bodies, let's face it, sometimes it feels like we're trying to solve a Rubik's Cube—blindfolded. Between deciphering the latest health trends and squeezing workouts into jam-packed schedules, staying active can seem like a chore reserved for superheroes. But what if I told you that weaving exercise into your life could be as enjoyable as your favourite Netflix binge? Yes, it's possible, and no, you don't need to morph into a marathon runner overnight. This chapter is about crafting a fitness routine that fits snugly into your life, not requiring you to bend over backward (unless that's part of your chosen workout).

THE FOUNDATION OF MOVEMENT: EXERCISE THAT FITS YOUR LIFE

Tailoring Exercise to Your Lifestyle

Creating an exercise routine that feels like a treat rather than a trial starts with a simple rule: tailor it to your lifestyle, not the other way around. Begin by assessing your daily routine. Are you a morning enthusiast who thrives by getting things done at dawn, or does the thought of that make you want to hit snooze until noon? Depending on your answer, you might slot in a brisk walk before breakfast or a calming yoga session after dinner. The trick is to anchor your exercise to existing habits. Perhaps you could pair a quick jog with your morning coffee run or do a dance workout right before your Favorite TV show starts. By piggybacking on the routines you already have, exercise feels less like an imposition and more like a natural part of your day.

But what about those days crammed with meetings, errands, and a to-do list longer than a CVS receipt? Enter the world of 'exercise snacks'. No, not granola bars, but mini workouts spread throughout the day. Think ten squats while waiting for the kettle to boil, calf raises when brushing your teeth, or a two-minute dance party with your kids in the living room. These snippets of activity add up, keeping your energy levels high and your body in motion without requiring dedicated gym time.

Overcoming Exercise Barriers

Let's tackle the twin hurdles of time constraints and motivational slumps. First up, time—or the lack of it. It's the most significant barrier for most of us, but as we explored with 'exercise snacks', every little bit counts. Also, consider high-intensity interval training (HIIT), where short bursts of high-energy exercise are followed by brief rest periods. Just 15 minutes can have a significant impact, boosting your heart health and metabolism.

As for motivation, let's make exercise irresistibly fun. Choose activities that make you feel like a kid on a playground—be it cycling, swimming, or a Zumba class. The more enjoy the activity, the less you'll view it as a chore. And here's a little secret: leverage the power of accountability. Partner with a friend, join a class, or involve your family. It's harder to bail on a workout when someone else is counting on you; plus, it's way more fun.

Variety is Key

Your body loves a challenge, and nothing says challenge quite like mixing things up. If your workout routine feels like Groundhog Day, it's time to inject some variety. Not only does this keep boredom at bay, but it also ensures you're working different muscle groups and energy systems. This week, it might be kickboxing and Pilates; next week, trail running and strength training. This approach enhances overall fitness and reduces the risk of injury from overuse. Plus, it keeps your metabolic rate guessing, which can be beneficial if weight management is one of your goals.

Measuring Progress Beyond the Scale

Now, let's talk about measuring success. If your fitness tracker or scale solely judges your progress, it's time to recalibrate your metrics. How you feel during and after workouts is a far more telling sign of your fitness journey. Do you have more energy? Are you sleeping better? Is climbing stairs less daunting? These qualitative measures are incredibly important. They remind you that exercise benefits your mind and mood just as much as it does your body, providing a fuller picture of your progress than numbers on a scale ever could.

Reflect and Adjust

Before we move on, take a moment to reflect on your current exercise habits. What's working for you? What's not? Use this insight to tweak and fine-tune your approach. Remember, the aim is to find joy in movement, to celebrate what your body can do, and to elevate your day-to-day life through the vibrant energy that physical activity brings. So, lace up your trusty training shoes, unroll your yoga mat, or grab that bike out of the garage—it's time to make exercise a delightfully integral part of your life, tailored just for you, without the need for a cape or superpowers.

SLEEP HYGIENE: CREATING A RESTFUL SANCTUARY

Let's talk about sleep, not just any sleep, but the rejuvenating, soul-soothing, cognitive-function-boosting kind of sleep. It's the unsung hero in the world of self-care, often shuffled to the bottom of our priority list, right under "sort sock drawer" and "learn to juggle." Yet, sleep is a critical component of our well-being, influencing everything from our mood and energy levels to our ability to make decisions and think clearly. It's like the operating system of our bodies; if it's glitchy, everything else tends to freeze up or malfunction.

Deep, quality sleep does more than make you feel less grumpy in the morning. It plays a pivotal role in brain health, particularly in storing memories and learning new information. During sleep, our brains are far from inactive; they are busily organizing and consolidating our memories, making sense of the day's experiences, and even solving problems that stumped us in daylight hours. This nighttime activity is crucial for neuroplasticity—the brain's incredible ability to reorganize itself by forming new neural connections. Good sleep doesn't just help you feel refreshed; it helps your brain reshape itself in ways that enhance cognitive function and emotional regulation.

The Essentials of Sleep Hygiene

Diving into sleep hygiene, we first encounter the cornerstone of consistency. Keeping a regular sleep schedule sets your body's internal clock to expect rest at certain times. Punctuality isn't just a virtue for meetings; it's crucial for your sleep, too. Aim to go to bed and wake up at the same time every day, yes, even on weekends. This regularity strengthens your sleep-wake cycle, making it easier to fall asleep and wake naturally.

Next, let's optimize your sleeping environment. Your bedroom should be a temple of tranquillity. Evaluate your space from a sensory perspective. Start with lighting: dim, soft lights help cue your body towards sleep, so consider swapping out those harsh, bright bulbs. Noise is next on the list. If external sounds are a bother, white noise machines or apps can mask interruptions. And let's not forget about temperature. Cooler rooms often support better sleep, so set your thermostat around 65 degrees Fahrenheit (18°C) to invite the sandman in.

Material comforts matter, too. Invest in a good-quality mattress and pillows that support your preferred sleeping position. Your bedding can be pivotal in your comfort levels, so choose breathable, natural fibres that help regulate temperature and keep you cozy through the night.

The Impact of Electronics

In our tech-saturated world, screens are often the last thing we see at night and the first in the morning. Yet, this habit is one of the biggest thieves of quality sleep. The blue light emitted by phones, tablets, and computers suppresses melatonin production—the hormone that tells your brain it's time to sleep. To combat this:

1. Institute an electronic curfew an hour before bed.
2. Swap out scrolling through social media or answering emails with winding down activities that don't involve screens, like reading a book or listening to soothing music.
3. If you must use devices, consider settings or apps that reduce blue light exposure in the evening.

Pre-sleep Rituals

Cultivating a pre-sleep ritual is like whispering to your body, "It's time to wind down now." This ritual can include anything that signals your body that sleep is imminent. Perhaps it's a warm bath infused with lavender, a scent known for its relaxing properties. Or maybe it's a series of gentle, restorative yoga poses followed by a few minutes of deep breathing exercises. What matters is that your ritual fits your preferences and is feasible to perform consistently. Make it something you look forward to, a personal treat at the end of each day, not a chore.

Dealing with Insomnia

Despite your best efforts, there might be nights where sleep eludes you. When insomnia strikes, it's important not to panic or try to force sleep, which can create anxiety and make falling asleep even harder. Instead, if you haven't fallen asleep after 20 minutes, leave your bedroom and engage in a quiet,non-stimulating activity. Avoid screens; perhaps try reading or listening to soft music until you feel sleepy.

Persistent insomnia, however, may require professional intervention. If sleepless nights become the norm rather than the exception, it might be time to consult a healthcare provider. Sometimes, insomnia can be a symptom of underlying health issues, and addressing these with professional help can restore your night's peace.

In rounding out our chat on sleep hygiene, remember that the goal here is to create conditions that allow sleep to come naturally and plentifully. It's about setting the stage for sleep with as much care as you'd prepare for a big day. After all, every good day begins the night before. So, here's to closing your eyes and drifting into dreamland with ease, embracing the night's embrace as the ultimate form of nightly self-care.

NUTRITIONAL SELF-CARE: MINDFUL EATING PRACTICES

In Chapter 1 we explored the concept of 'eating for happiness', considering the importance of the nutritional value and impact of what we put into our bodies at mealtimes. Now we are exploring how we can benefit from mindful eating practices. Transitioning into mindful eating practices isn't just about slowly chewing your food or avoiding distractions while you eat, those these are good starts. Imagine transforming every meal into an experience for your senses and a health boost for your body. Yes, it's entirely possible and surprisingly simple with mindful eating. This isn't about strict diets or eating only kale and quinoa. Mindful eating is about fully experiencing your food's flavours, textures, and joys. It's about slowing down, paying attention, and savouring every bite, which not only enhances your eating experience but also can improve digestion and reduce overeating. To start, try this: at your next meal, eliminate distractions. Turn off the TV, put away your phone, and just focus on your food. Notice the colour, smell, and texture. Chew slowly, and really taste each mouthful. It's like turning a simple meal into a sensory adventure.

Now, let's talk about tuning into your body's signals. Our bodies are wise; they know when they need food and when they've had enough. But in our fast-paced world, it's easy to miss these cues. We eat because it's lunchtime, not because we're hungry or keep munching even when we're full. Listening to your body means pausing before you eat to ask yourself, "Am I really hungry?" And then, while eating, regularly check in to assess if you're satisfied. This might mean setting down your fork between bites or taking a small break midway through the meal to decide if you want to continue eating. This practice helps prevent overeating and ensures you eat for nourishment rather than out of boredom or emotion.

Cooking at home is another pillar of nutritional self-care. There's something inherently nurturing about preparing your own meals. It's a chance to connect with the food that sustains you and to control what goes into your body. Start simple. You don't need to be a gourmet chef to cook nutritious meals. Begin with recipes that require minimal ingredients and steps. Think stir-fried veggies, simple salads, or grilled proteins. Involve your senses in the process —enjoy the sizzle of garlic in the pan or the vibrant colours of fresh produce. Make your kitchen a stress-free zone where creativity meets health. Cooking can be incredibly meditative and a great way to decompress after a long day.

By embracing these practices, you turn every meal into an opportunity for health and pleasure. You learn to appreciate the subtleties of flavours, to listen to your body's needs, and to take active control of your nutrition. This isn't just eating; it's a way to honour your body and mind, meal by meal, in the most delicious way possible.

HYDRATION AND HEALTH: THE UNSUNG HERO OF SELF-CARE

Water, my friend, is not just something that fills the kettle for our tea or the tub for a soak. It's the lifeblood of our cells, the transporter of nutrients, and the cleaner of toxins. Hydration plays a pivotal role in everything from maintaining our brain function to keeping our muscles moving smoothly. Think of your body as a high-tech factory; water is the oil that keeps all the gears running smoothly. Without it, things start to grind, overheat, and eventually, break down. Cognitive functions like concentration and memory can become as sluggish as a Monday morning without coffee; physical performance might feel like you're wading through molasses.

Now, let's talk about dehydration, which can sneak up on you like the plot twist in your favourite thriller. It often masquerades as fatigue, hunger, or just a bad mood. Recognizing the signs is crucial —things like headaches, dry mouth, and darker urine are your body's less-than-subtle hints that you need to sip more. But waiting until you're parched before you reach for a glass of water is like waiting until your car runs out of gas before you decide to fill up; it's a little too late and definitely not advisable. The trick is to keep your hydration levels steady throughout the day. Carry a water bottle with you as if it's your new best friend. Set reminders on your phone if you tend to forget or tie them to daily tasks—drink a glass of water before each meal, one after each trip to the restroom, and a sip every time a commercial pops up during your TV time.

If plain water bores you to yawns, let's jazz it up. Infusing water with fruits, herbs, or cucumbers isn't just for spa guests. You can do this at home, and it's as easy as tossing your favourite combinations into a pitcher. Imagine sipping on cucumber-mint water or a berry-rosemary concoction. Not only does it look pretty in your glass, but the subtle flavours make hydration feel like a treat rather than a chore. For a warm twist, especially in cooler weather, consider herbal teas. They count towards your fluid intake and can be a soothing, caffeine-free boost to your hydration habits.

Balancing your fluid intake is like being a DJ for your body, mixing the right tracks to keep the vibe going. It's not just about water; all fluids count, but some are definitely better than others. While coffee and tea are fine in moderation, they shouldn't be your primary hydration sources since caffeine can have a diuretic effect. And sugary drinks? They're like that one hit wonder song: fun in the moment but not really something you want on repeat. Instead, focus on water, herbal teas, and other low-sugar beverages to maintain optimal hydration. Also, consider your activity level. If you're hitting the gym, running, or even chasing a toddler around the park, your body will need more fluids to compensate for what's lost in sweat. Listen to your body; it's the best DJ you've got and will let you know when you need to turn up the hydration beats.

Managing your hydration is an art that colours the canvas of your health with vibrant hues of vitality. It's not just about avoiding the pitfalls of dehydration but embracing the fluid balance that keeps you feeling energized, focused, and at your best. So, drink up, my dear, and let every sip channel sparkle, energy, and life into your every day. Remember, staying hydrated is not just a drop in the bucket; it's the whole ocean of your well-being, keeping you afloat and sailing smoothly through your day.

THE HEALING POWER OF NATURE: OUTDOOR ACTIVITIES FOR WELL-BEING

When was the last time you stepped outside, took a deep breath, and felt your worries lighten just a tad as the fresh air filled your lungs? There's something undeniably therapeutic about nature. It's not just about the scenic views or the break from the urban jungle; it's about reconnecting with the earth and rediscovering a rhythm that often gets lost in the shuffle of daily life. Nature is a natural therapy in its serene and boundless forms, offering benefits that span the spectrum from physical enhancements to profound mental relief.

Nature as Therapy

The concept of nature as a healing agent isn't new. Civilizations have recognized the calming and restorative effects of spending time in natural settings for centuries. Today, science has begun to catch up, providing evidence that time outdoors can lower blood pressure, reduce stress hormones, and enhance feelings of well-being. When you immerse yourself in nature, it's not just a walk in the park; it's an engagement with a living environment that promotes health through clean air, tranquil sounds, and visually soothing landscapes. This interaction boosts serotonin levels—the feel-good neurotransmitter—and reduces cortisol, a stress-related hormone. Even a few minutes spent under the canopy of trees or by a flowing stream can recalibrate your mood and improve your overall health.

Accessible Outdoor Activities

You don't need to be near a majestic mountain range or a sprawling forest to integrate nature into your self-care routine. Urban parks, community gardens, or even your backyard can be the backdrop for your green retreat. For those who find themselves in concrete-heavy environments, consider creating a green space on your balcony with potted plants or frequenting a local botanical garden. Activities can be as simple as a daily walk in your nearest park, bird watching, or having a picnic with friends or family under the open sky. Every city has pockets of nature if you look closely. Even routine paths can be transformed into mindful nature walks that focus on absorbing the surrounding natural elements, turning a simple walk into a rejuvenating experience.

The Concept of Forest Bathing

One of the most profound ways to connect with nature is through the practice of forest bathing, or "Shinrin-yoku," a term coined in Japan in the 1980s. This practice involves:

- Slowly walking through a forest.
- Soaking in the atmosphere.
- Taking in the environment through all your senses.

It's not about covering miles or reaching physical peaks; it's about letting the natural world fill your senses. The scientifically proven benefits of forest bathing include reduced stress, increased energy levels, and improved sleep, largely attributed to inhaling phytoncides—natural oils within wood that trees emit to protect themselves from germs and insects. These substances have antibacterial and antifungal qualities, which can boost the human immune system. A forest bathing session isn't just a walk; it's a medicinal immersion in the forest's healing powers.

Engaging the Senses

To deepen the therapeutic effects of your time outdoors, engage all your senses. See if you can identify the shades of green you see or the variety of bird calls you hear. Touch the textures of leaves, the roughness of tree bark, or the coolness of a stream. Smell the earth after a rain or the fragrance of wildflowers. If safe, taste the freshness of the air or the sweetness of a berry picked from a bush. This sensory approach enriches your experience and anchors you in the present moment, which is a core aspect of mindfulness practices. It transforms a simple outdoor activity into a rich, immersive experience that can rejuvenate mind and body.

As you incorporate these elements into your life, remember that the aim is to find peace and restoration through the simple act of being in nature. Whether it's a morning jog in the park, a weekend hike, or an afternoon in your garden, each moment spent in the embrace of the natural world is a step towards a healthier, happier you. So next time you feel overwhelmed or disconnected, step outside— your green therapist is waiting, ready to soothe, heal, and inspire.

INTEGRATING TRADITIONAL AND ALTERNATIVE MEDICINE

When it comes to maintaining our health, sometimes thinking outside the conventional medicine box brings us into a world of healing that is both ancient and refreshingly innovative. Integrating traditional and alternative medicine into our self-care routines can be like adding a pinch of exotic spice to a trusted recipe—it might just be the secret ingredient we've been missing. Whether it's the targeted pressure of acupuncture easing the tension in your shoulders or a soothing herbal tea that calms your busy mind, combining traditional practices with modern medicine can create a uniquely effective health regimen.

Complementary Approaches to Health

Imagine your healthcare plan as a well-orchestrated symphony. Each element, from traditional medicine to alternative therapies, plays a distinct part. Still, together, they create a harmony that enhances your overall well-being. For instance, while conventional medicine might treat your chronic pain with medications, adding acupuncture could reduce the pain further and decrease reliance on pharmaceuticals. Similarly, integrating massage therapy can improve circulation and mobility, complementing physical therapy or post-surgical recovery processes. This holistic approach doesn't just treat symptoms; it aims to enhance your entire body's functioning and, significantly, your quality of life.

Navigating through the myriad options of alternative therapies might seem daunting at first. With practices ranging from ancient Ayurveda to modern biofeedback, how do you know where to begin? Start by identifying what you want to improve or heal in your body. Are you seeking pain relief, stress reduction, or perhaps a boost in your immune system? Once you have a clear goal, research which therapies align with your needs. For instance, you might explore yoga or meditation if stress reduction is your goal. Consider treatments like chiropractic adjustments or herbal supplements for physical ailments like inflammation or muscle tension. Always check the credentials and reviews of the practitioners and look for those who are certified and have reputable practices.

Safety and Efficacy

While the allure of alternative therapies can be strong, especially when traditional treatments haven't provided the desired relief, it's crucial to approach them with a discerning mind. Safety first— always ensure the therapies you consider are safe and evidence-supported. It's wise to consult with your healthcare provider before beginning any new treatment, especially if you have underlying health conditions or are taking medications that could interact with herbal remedies. Your doctor can help you assess various therapies' safety and potential efficacy within your overall health plan.

For instance, while herbal supplements can offer significant benefits, they can also interact with medications and impact their effectiveness. A professional can help you navigate these waters safely. Additionally, look for scientific research or clinical trials that back the efficacy of the treatments you're considering. While many alternative therapies have centuries of anecdotal support, scientific validation can help you make informed decisions.

As we wrap up this exploration of traditional and alternative medicine, remember that the ultimate goal is to find a balanced, effective approach to your health. Whether through an acupuncturist's precise needles, the massage therapist's deep tissue manipulation, or the healing herbs prescribed by a naturopath, each modality offers unique benefits that can support and enhance your well-being. Thoughtfully integrating these practices into your health regimen opens the door to a more vibrant, healthful life, tuning your body's natural healing abilities to their optimal frequency. Now, as we turn the page from the physical realms of health, let's delve deeper into the emotional and mental landscapes that shape our well-being in the next chapter.

Reflection Section – Fine Tuning Physical Elements of Self-Care

"I go to nature to be soothed, healed and have my senses put in order."

JOHN BURROUGHS

In this chapter, we delved into:

- The significance of <u>physical activity</u> and movement for our wellness.
- The impact of <u>sleep quality</u> on our self-care practices.
- The importance of <u>staying hydrated</u> for our overall health.
- The advantages of practicing <u>mindful eating.</u>

- The necessity of <u>integrating nature</u> into our self-care rituals.
- The integration of <u>alternative and traditional medicine</u> into our self-care strategies.

In the coming days, dedicate moments to engage with the journal prompts provided. Reflect on the insights gained from this chapter and consider how they can be woven into the fabric of your personal self-care.

Exercise:

- What physical activities did I engage in this week and how did they make me feel both during and after?
- Are there any barriers that prevent me from exercising regularly, and how can I address these obstacles?

Sleep

- How would I rate the quality of my sleep over the past week and what factors might have influenced it?
- What changes can I make to my evening routine to improve my sleep hygiene and overall quality of sleep?

Hydration

- How do I feel on days when I drink enough water compared to days when I don't?
- What strategies can I implement to consistently stay hydrated throughout the day?

Mindful Eating

- What are my eating patterns and how do they reflect my emotional or physical needs?
- How does the food I choose affect my mood and energy levels?

Connecting with Nature

- How often do I spend time in natural settings, and what impact does this have on my well-being?
- What can I do to make nature a more regular part of my life?

Alternative and Traditional Medicine

- What experience have I had with alternative or traditional medicines and how have they impacted my health?
- How open am I to incorporating different medical practices into my wellness routine, and what might I want to explore?

CHAPTER 4 (DAYS 16 – 20)
EMOTIONAL AND MENTAL WELLNESS

I magine your mind as a bustling city. There's the Memory District, bustling with constant activity; the Emotion Quarter, where the mood changes; and the serene Mindfulness Park, where peace and calm reign supreme. Like any thriving city, your mental landscape needs some maintenance to keep everything running smoothly. That's where emotional and mental wellness comes into play, helping to balance the hustle and bustle with moments of quiet reflection and rejuvenation.

MINDFULNESS IN PRACTICE: DAILY HABITS FOR INNER PEACE

Incorporating Mindfulness into Everyday Life

Mindfulness might sound like a serene retreat on a mountaintop. Still, it's actually as accessible as your spice rack, available to sprinkle a little calm throughout your day. It's about being present in the moment, fully engaged in whatever you're doing, whether washing dishes, driving, or sipping coffee. This practice isn't about adding more to your to-do list but changing how you approach your daily tasks. So, how about turning your morning shower into a practice of mindfulness? Feel the water's temperature, the soap's scent, and the droplets' sound. This isn't just washing; it's being present, transforming a routine shower into a refreshing mental cleanse.

Another simple practice is the "Mindful Pause." Before starting a new task, take a moment to breathe and center yourself. This can be as brief as three deep breaths. It's like hitting the reset button between activities, clearing your mental palate before you dive into the next part of your day. It's astonishing how these small pauses can shift your perspective, helping you approach tasks with a fresher, calmer mindset.

Mindful Movement: Using gentle forms of exercise, like yoga or tai chi, to cultivate both physical and mental well-being.

Mindful movement practices such as yoga and tai chi are not just exercises for your body but feasts for your mind. They combine physical movement with an awareness of breath and the present moment, making them powerful tools for cultivating tranquillity. Imagine performing a series of yoga poses with a focus not just on alignment but on how each stretch feels in your body. Or picture yourself practicing tai chi in a park, your movements slow and deliberate, synchronized with your breathing. These practices strengthen the body while calming the mind, providing a double dose of self-care.

Breathing Techniques: Specific breathing exercises that can quickly bring a sense of calm and focus

Let's dive into a simple yet profound technique: the 4-7-8 breathing exercise. Here's how it goes:

- Breathe in through your nose for 4 seconds.
- Hold that breath for 7 seconds.
- Exhale slowly through your mouth for 8 seconds.

This breathing pattern acts like a mental broom, sweeping away stress and returning your focus to the present. It's a technique you can pull out of your self-care toolkit whether you're about to enter a stressful meeting or winding down for the night. The beauty of breathing exercises is that they're discreet, flexible, and incredibly effective, offering a quick mental reset wherever and whenever you need it.

The Role of Meditation: Introducing different forms of meditation as foundational practices for mental wellness

Meditation is often hailed as a pathway to peace, and it's not just poetic language. The benefits range from lowered stress levels and reduced anxiety to enhanced attention and better memory. If you're new to meditation, the practice might seem daunting, but it's really about simplicity. Start with guided meditations, which are available through apps or online. These can lead you through the process, helping you focus and redirect your thoughts as you practice. As you grow more comfortable, you might explore other forms, such as mindfulness meditation, which involves observing your thoughts and feelings without judgment, or loving-kindness meditation, which focuses on developing feelings of goodwill towards yourself and others. Regular meditation can be a sanctuary for your mind, a place you can visit daily to shed stress and gather peace.

As we explore these practices, remember that the goal isn't to empty your mind or achieve some moment of enlightenment after a single session. It's about building a relationship with the present moment, training your mind to focus on the here and now, and finding peace within yourself, regardless of the chaos that might swirl around you. These practices are tools for coping and thriving, allowing you to cultivate a state of calm and clarity that enhances every aspect of your life. So, as you continue on your day, remember to breathe, move mindfully, and give yourself permission to pause and be present. Your mental cityscape will thank you for becoming a more peaceful, productive place to live.

NAVIGATING STRESS: TECHNIQUES FOR IMMEDIATE RELIEF

Let's face it, stress is like that one guest who shows up uninvited to every party, eats all your snacks, and doesn't get the hint to leave. While some stress can motivate, too much can crash your mental peace party. So, what's a gal to do when stress overstays its welcome? First up, let's talk about progressive muscle relaxation. This method might sound like a new yoga trend but is actually a tried-and-true stress buster. Picture this: you're lying in a quiet room, and you begin by tensing the muscles in your toes for about five seconds and then relaxing them for 30 seconds. You then work your way up the body, tensing and relaxing each muscle group. It's like sending a wave of relaxation through your body, which can help melt away stress like butter on a hot pancake.

Next on the stress-busting menu is visualization. This isn't about daydreaming your stress away (though wouldn't that be nice?) but rather about using your imagination to transport you to a calmer, happier place. Close your eyes and picture a scene that soothes you —maybe lying on a sun-drenched beach, listening to the waves lap against the shore, or sitting in a cozy mountain cabin by a crackling fire. Engage all your senses to make the experience feel as real as possible. The beauty of visualization is that your brain often can't distinguish between real and vividly imagined experiences, so it reacts to these peaceful images by dialing down your stress levels.

Creating a Stress-Response Plan

Having a game plan for when stress hits the red zone can be a total game-changer. Start by identifying your stress signals—maybe your heart races, your breathing quickens, or you get that knotted feeling in your stomach. Recognizing these signs early on can help you take proactive steps before stress spirals. Create a list of go-to activities that you know help you unwind. This could be anything from taking a brisk walk or doing a quick meditation session to calling a friend for a chat. Keep this list on your phone or somewhere easily accessible to turn to it when the pressure is mounting. Think of this plan as your stress emergency kit—it's there to help you regain control and restore peace.

The Importance of Play

As adults, we often undervalue play, relegating it to the 'unnecessary' or 'frivolous' corners of our lives. But reintroducing play and leisure into your routine can be a powerful antidote to stress. Play sparks joy, unleashes creativity, and can even boost your problem-solving abilities. It might be as simple as dancing around your living room to your favorite tunes, playing a board game with your family, or painting just for fun. These playful activities can distract you from your worries, bring a sense of lightness and spontaneity to your day, and remind you that life isn't all about to-do lists and responsibilities.

Harnessing the Power of Music

Never underestimate the power of a good beat. Music is not just the background noise to our lives; it can be a powerful therapeutic tool for managing stress and regulating emotions. Music can shift your mood dramatically, whether it's classical symphonies that soothe your soul or upbeat pop songs that make you want to dance out the stress. Create a playlist of tunes that lift your spirits or calm your mind and keep it handy for stress emergencies. Sometimes, it takes just a few minutes of getting lost in the music to reset your stress levels and regain your groove.

As you weave these strategies into the fabric of your daily life, remember that managing stress is not about eliminating it completely—let's be realistic; life throws curveballs. It's about developing the tools and techniques to catch those balls and throw them back with less chaos and more confidence. So, the next time stress tries to crash your party, greet it with a smile because you've got a playlist to dance to, a beach to imagine, and a game plan that turns stress into a guest who can make life a little more interesting.

DECONSTRUCTING ANXIETY: TOOLS FOR TRANQUILLITY

Anxiety, that jittery guest at the party of your mind, may seem like it has a permanent invitation, but let's chat about how you can start reclaiming your mental space. Understanding the roots of anxiety is like pulling up the weeds in your garden; it's crucial for maintaining your mental landscape. Anxiety doesn't just appear out of nowhere—it's often the result of a complex interplay of genetic factors, life experiences, and daily stresses. It might stem from an overactive fight-or-flight response or a history of stressful events that have left you on edge. By pinpointing the origins of your anxiety, whether it's a learned response to stress or a side effect of a hectic lifestyle, you can tailor your approach to managing it more effectively.

Now, let's delve into the realm of cognitive behavioral techniques, a powerful set of tools in your mental health toolkit. Cognitive

Behavioral Therapy (CBT) is like having a roadmap that helps you navigate the often-tricky terrain of your thoughts and emotions. It's based on the idea that our thoughts, feelings, and behaviors are interconnected and that changing one can change the others. For instance, if you often think you cannot handle your responsibilities, CBT techniques can help you challenge and reshape this thought. By practicing reframing your thoughts to be more positive and realistic, you can reduce the anxiety these negative thoughts often produce. It's about training your mind to approach problems in a new, more constructive way. Consider trying a simple CBT exercise: write down a recurring anxious thought and then challenge it by writing down evidence that contradicts it. This practice can help weaken the hold that irrational fears may have on your emotions.

Shifting gears, let's talk about physical activity, a surprisingly effective but often underestimated player in managing anxiety. We have already considered the importance of incorporating activity and movement into our self-care plan, but did you know that regular physical activity can also be like hitting a reset button on your stress levels? It helps release endorphins, as we know, those feel-good neurotransmitters that act as natural painkillers and mood lifters. But here's the kicker—it also helps burn off accumulated stress hormones, like adrenaline and cortisol, which can fuel anxiety. Whether it's a brisk walk, a run, or a session at the gym, making exercise a regular part of your routine can significantly reduce anxiety levels. And the beauty of it? The benefits are both immediate and long-term, helping not just to manage acute anxiety but to build resilience against future stress.

Lastly, let's not overlook the role of nutrition in managing anxiety. I know, we have focussed on nutrition earlier in our self-care journey; however, here, we view it specifically through the lens of managing anxiety. What you put on your plate can influence how you feel in your head. Certain foods can exacerbate anxiety symptoms, while others can help tame them. For instance, caffeine and sugar, while providing a quick energy boost, can also lead to a crash in mood and energy levels, potentially increasing anxiety.

On the other hand, a diet rich in whole grains, vegetables, and omega-3 fatty acids can support brain health and improve mood stability. Consider incorporating foods like salmon, avocados, and almonds, which contain nutrients that can help calm the nervous system and enhance your overall mental well-being. It's not just about cutting out the bad stuff; it's about filling your diet with nourishing and calming foods.

By understanding the roots of your anxiety, employing cognitive strategies to manage anxious thoughts, staying active, and eating right, you create a comprehensive strategy that addresses anxiety on all fronts. Each step moves toward tranquillity, a way to quiet the mind and soothe the spirit. So, the next time anxiety knocks on your door, remember you have the tools to answer calmly and confidently.

CULTIVATING POSITIVE EMOTIONS: ACTIVITIES TO BOOST YOUR MOOD

Let's talk happiness—the real, laugh-out-loud, feel-it-in-your-toes kind. It's like the perfect walk on the beach, or in your local park, on a sunny Sunday morning. But in the hustle of everyday life, finding those blissful moments can sometimes feel like searching for a lost earring in a ball pit. However, the field of positive psychology offers us some shiny tools to help dig out those joyful moments more frequently. At its core, positive psychology focuses on what makes life most worth living, emphasizing happiness, well-being, and flourishing. So, how do we sprinkle more of this shiny happiness dust into our daily routines?

First up, let's explore the realm of Gratitude. Now, I know you might be thinking, "Gratitude? Isn't that just saying thank you?" But it's so much more. Gratitude is about recognizing the good in our lives, and research shows it has a powerful impact on our emotional well-being. It can lift our spirits, boost our resilience, and even strengthen our immune systems. But hold on, we will explore the concept and power of Gratitude in depth in the next section of this chapter.

Next, let's dive briefly again into the warmth of human connections, building on what we have learnt about the science of social bonds in Chapter 1. Our relationships are like cozy, emotional blankets—wrapping us in comfort, security, and joy. But maintaining these connections requires effort, especially when life gets busy. To keep the emotional warmth flowing remember to:

1. Actively reach out to friends and family.
2. Schedule regular meet-ups, whether it's a coffee date or a video chat.
3. Share your ups and downs, listen to their stories, and laugh over memories.

These interactions are not just social obligations; they are lifelines to emotional health, reinforcing your sense of belonging and happiness.

Now, finding purpose in the every day might sound like a tall order—like finding a needle in a haystack. But it's really about finding meaning in the ordinary. Every task, no matter how small, has significance. Whether preparing a meal, helping a colleague, or organizing a space in your home, approach these activities with intention. Ask yourself, "What value does this bring?" or "How does this enrich my life or the lives of others?" This mindset can transform mundane tasks into sources of joy and satisfaction, infusing your daily routine with purpose and happiness.

In weaving these threads of Gratitude, connection, and purpose into the fabric of your daily life, you create a tapestry rich with happiness and contentment. So, as you move through your day, remember that happiness isn't a destination. It's a series of moments and choices that, when woven together, create a colorful, joyful life. Embrace these practices and watch your days sparkle with more frequent flashes of joy, reminding you that happiness, like a perfect cup of coffee, is most enjoyable when savored slowly and with intention.

EMOTIONAL JOURNALING: WRITING YOUR WAY TO WELL-BEING

Let's talk about emotional journaling, not just as a diary of daily events, but as a deep-sea dive into the colorful coral reefs of your emotions. Think of it as your personal therapist, tucked neatly into the pages of a notebook, always ready to listen without judgment. Journaling is a potent tool for emotional expression and processing. It can be a safe space where you spill out frustrations, celebrate joys, and navigate the complex map of your feelings. Putting pen to paper forces you to slow down and engage with your thoughts and emotions on a deeper level, offering clarity that the hustle of everyday life often clouds.

Consider this: each time you journal, you embark on a mini-adventure into the depths of your mind, discovering hidden treasures of insight and understanding along the way. This practice can lead to significant breakthroughs in understanding and reacting to life's challenges. It's about more than just venting; it's about transforming your relationship with your emotions. By regularly communicating with yourself through your journal, you develop a stronger, more compassionate internal dialogue. You might start to notice patterns in your emotional responses that were previously fogged by the chaos of daily life. This awareness can be incredibly empowering, allowing you to reshape your narrative and approach life with a renewed sense of control and optimism.

Guided Journal Prompts: Providing prompts to help explore feelings, challenges, and aspirations

If staring at a blank page feels as daunting as starting a new workout routine, guided journal prompts can be the warm-up you need. These prompts act as starting blocks for your thoughts, guiding you through introspection. For instance, try prompts like, "What situation made me feel anxious this week and why?" or "What brought me joy today?" These questions can help steer your writing towards meaningfully exploring your feelings and experiences. They spark a dialogue with yourself that might otherwise be drowned out by life's noise. Over time, as you respond to these prompts, you'll start to uncover deeper truths about your desires, fears, and joys, which can illuminate paths to personal growth and emotional healing.

Creative Expression: Encouraging the use of art, music, or poetry in journaling to deepen emotional exploration

Integrating art, music, or poetry into your journaling can enrich the experience for those who think in colours rather than words. This isn't about crafting a masterpiece; it's about using these mediums to express what might be too complex or daunting to capture with words alone. Draw a picture representing how you feel about a recent life event, write a poem about a challenge you're facing, or attach a song lyric that resonates with your current mood. These creative additions can provide new dimensions to your journaling practice, making it a richer, more engaging dialogue with your inner self. They bring texture to the tapestry of your thoughts and emotions, offering insights that might not emerge through words alone.

Overcoming Journaling Blocks: Tips for getting started with journaling and making it a consistent practice

Finally, let's address the elephant in the room—journaling blocks. Like any good habit, starting and maintaining a journaling practice can come with challenges. If you struggle to write regularly, schedule a specific time each day dedicated to journaling, even if it's just five minutes. Treat it like a crucial appointment with yourself. Keep your journal and a pen in a convenient, visible place to remind you of this commitment. If you're stuck on what to write, describe your day, how you felt about different events, or what you're looking forward to tomorrow. Remember, the goal is to connect with yourself - your feelings, thoughts, realizations, concerns and triumphs. As you ease into this practice, you'll find that the words begin to flow more freely, turning journaling into a cherished and insightful part of your daily routine.

Emotional journaling is a journey of self-discovery and healing that starts with a single word and grows into a comprehensive narrative of your personal growth. It's a practice that invites honesty, nurtures self-compassion, and fosters an in-depth understanding of your life story. So, grab that journal and let the pages become a canvas for your thoughts and emotions—a space where you can write your way to well-being.

THE POWER OF GRATITUDE: TRANSFORMING THOUGHT PATTERNS

Cultivating an Attitude of Gratitude

Now, let's continue on our path to Gratitude, and understanding how it can enrich our experience of self-care. Imagine flipping a switch in your brain that transforms how you view your day-to-day experiences. That's the power of cultivating an attitude of Gratitude. It's like wearing rose-colored glasses, but better because the effects are not just about seeing the world more positively but fundamentally enhancing your mental health. Gratitude shifts your focus from what's missing to what's present, from the empty half of the glass to the overflowing half. Think of it as a mental muscle that, when flexed regularly, strengthens your overall emotional resilience, making you less susceptible to the stresses that life throws your way.

But how do you develop this mindset? Start by setting aside a few minutes daily to reflect on things you're thankful for. It could be as profound as appreciating your health or as simple as a warm cup of coffee on a chilly morning. The key is consistency. Like any habit, the more you practice Gratitude, the more natural it becomes. Over time, this practice not only boosts your mood and outlook but also decreases the likelihood of experiencing prolonged periods of sadness or depression. Researchers have found that Gratitude can significantly impact neurotransmitter systems linked to emotions, enhancing feelings of joy and contentment. By cultivating Gratitude, you're essentially wiring your brain to lean towards positivity, making it a formidable ally in the quest for emotional well-being.

Gratitude Practices

To weave Gratitude more deeply into your life, consider integrating specific practices that reinforce this positive habit. One effective method is keeping a gratitude journal. Write down three things that went well during the day each night and your role in making them happen. This exercise helps you find joy in everyday moments. It reinforces your sense of agency in creating positive outcomes in your life. Another powerful practice is writing gratitude letters. Think of someone who has significantly impacted your life, and write them a detailed letter expressing your thanks. You can choose to send it or simply keep it as a reminder of the positive forces in your life. These practices don't just amplify your happiness; they often have a ripple effect, enhancing the positivity in your relationships and broader social interactions.

The Ripple Effect of Gratitude

The beauty of Gratitude is that it doesn't just beautify your inner world; it enhances your external world, too. Expressing gratitude, whether through words, actions, or simply a smile, can significantly improve your relationships. It creates a positive cycle of kindness and appreciation that can transform workplace dynamics, deepen friendships, and strengthen family bonds. For instance, thanking colleagues for their help on a project makes them feel valued. It often leads to a more collaborative and supportive work environment. Similarly, showing appreciation for your partner's everyday actions can deepen your connection, making your relationship more fulfilling. This ripple effect of Gratitude can turn your social circle into a supportive network where positivity and cooperation thrive, creating a healthier, happier community around you.

Overcoming Negativity Bias

Our brains tend to focus more on negative experiences than positive ones. This survival mechanism historically kept us safe from threats. However, in today's world, this negativity bias can lead us to overlook the good in our lives, contributing to stress and unhappiness. Gratitude directly challenges this bias by refocusing our attention on the positive aspects of our lives, helping to balance our emotional landscape. Each act of Gratitude is like a weight on the positive side of the scale, tipping it away from negativity and towards a more balanced, joyful outlook. Over time, this practice can transform your thought patterns, making positivity a more automatic response and allowing you to handle life's challenges with greater ease and resilience.

As we wrap up this exploration into the transformative power of Gratitude, remember that each small act of appreciation is a step towards a more joyous and resilient life. By regularly practicing Gratitude, you not only enhance your own well-being but also contribute to a more positive environment around you. It's a simple, powerful tool that can dramatically shift your perspective, turning everyday moments into opportunities for happiness and connection. So, as you move forward, take a moment to reflect on the good in your life, to express thanks, and to cultivate an atmosphere of Gratitude. Your mind, your relationships, and your world will be all the richer for it.

As we close this chapter on emotional and mental wellness, we carry the tools and insights to survive and thrive in our emotional landscapes. From mindfulness to stress management, from understanding anxiety to fostering happiness, and finally, to cultivating a transformative attitude of Gratitude, we are equipped to navigate the complexities of our emotions with grace and positivity. Let these strategies guide you as you explore, understand, and nurture your emotional well-being. In the next chapter, we will delve into the social dimensions of self-care, exploring how our relationships and social interactions can further enhance our journey toward a balanced and joyful life.

 Reflection Section - Positive affirmations

What You Think, You Become.

If you're new to the practice of positive affirmations, there's no better time to start than now. For those already familiar, this is a perfect opportunity to refresh your collection and discover new affirmations to elevate your self-care routine.

Positive affirmations are powerful statements that reinforce a woman's sense of self-worth, confidence, and potential. These affirmations are tools to combat self-doubt, negativity, and stress, fostering a mindset brimming with positivity and resilience. Here are a few examples of positive affirmations tailored for women:

- I am a strong and confident woman
- I have everything I need to succeed

- I am perfect just the way I am
- I trust the journey of my life and know that everything happens for a reason
- I am grateful for all the blessings in my life and choose to focus on the good

Now, embark on a journey to discover your top 10 affirmations. Explore various websites, peruse through books in your collection, seek recommendations from friends and family, or craft your own unique statements. After selecting them, document these affirmations in your journal, jot them down on sticky notes, and place them where you can see them every day to weave them seamlessly into your daily routine.

Here are a few websites to get you started:

- The Inner Tune
- The Good Body
- Daily Motivation Site

And to help you continue your affirmations journey, perhaps consider using an app which can send you daily affirmations. Here are some apps for you to explore:

- ThinkUp: Positive Affirmations
- Louise Hay Affirmation Meditations
- Shine
- Grateful
- Instar Affirmation Writer

Thank you for reading "Master Self-Care for Wise Women" by Nonie Adams! Your feedback is incredibly valuable to us. We would love to hear about your experience with the book.

Why Your Review Matters

Your review helps others discover the benefits of self-care and understand how this book can guide them on their journey. Sharing your thoughts can inspire and encourage others to take steps towards a healthier, happier life.

> *"There is no exercise better for the heart than reaching down and lifting people up."*
>
> JOHN HOLMES

How to Leave a Review

- Reflect on Your Journey: What did you find most helpful? How has your self-care routine changed?
- Be Honest and Specific: Your genuine thoughts and specific examples will help others see the practical benefits.
- Keep it Simple: A few sentences about your experience can make a big difference!

Sample Review

"I loved how 'Master Self-Care for Wise Women' broke down self-care into manageable daily tasks. The practical tips and short, easy-to-follow chapters made it simple to incorporate self-care into my busy life. Highly recommend!"

How to Leave Your Review

Simply scan the QR code below to leave your review:

Thank you for taking the time to share your thoughts and for being part of our community of wise women embracing self-care!

Warm regards,

Nonie Adams

CHAPTER 5 (DAYS 21 – 25)
SOCIAL SELF-CARE AND CONNECTION

I magine your social life as a garden. Just like any vibrant garden thrives on quality soil, sunlight, and water, your social well-being blossoms with laughter, shared memories, and supportive conversations. In this chapter, we're going to get our hands dirty in the delightful dirt of building and nurturing friendships that enrich your soil and make your personal ecosystem one of joy and resilience.

BUILDING ON OUR UNDERSTANDING OF FRIENDSHIPS

We've already discussed the critical role friendships play in our self-care journey, covering:

- The significance of friendships and their essential place in our self-care routines.
- Techniques for forging new friendships, including ways to meet others and establish authentic connections.
- Strategies for strengthening existing friendships with shared experiences and reciprocal support.

With this foundation, let's delve into additional facets of friendships that significantly influence our self-care practices.

Overcoming Social Anxiety: Techniques for Managing Feelings of Anxiety in Social Situations to Enable More Fulfilling Interactions

Social anxiety can turn the prospect of socializing into an overwhelming ordeal. If you find yourself fretting over upcoming social interactions, start with small, manageable steps. Begin with environments where you feel most comfortable, perhaps with close friends or small groups. Practice simple social skills like maintaining eye contact, smiling, and initiating small talk. Deep breathing or mindfulness techniques can also help calm your nerves before and during social events. Remember, it's perfectly okay to communicate your feelings with friends—they can be your allies in helping you navigate social settings more comfortably.

Interactive Element: Journaling Prompt

To deepen your understanding and practice of building and nurturing friendships, here's a reflective journaling prompt: Write about a friend who has positively impacted your life. What qualities do they possess that you value? How do they make you feel seen and heard? Reflecting on these questions can not only deepen your appreciation for this friendship but can also illuminate what qualities you may seek or cultivate in new friendships.

In the rich soil of social connections, every interaction has the potential to plant seeds of joy, growth, and mutual support. As you water these seeds with attention and care, watch as your garden of friendships blossoms, transforming your social ecosystem into a vibrant source of life and joy.

COMMUNICATING NEEDS: HOW TO ASK FOR SUPPORT

Let's face it, asking for help can sometimes feel as though you're admitting defeat, like you're signaling to the world that you've lost your superhero cape and can't possibly manage everything on your plate. But here's the twist: recognizing and expressing your needs is actually a superpower. It's about understanding yourself well enough to know when it's time to reach out, and it's about trusting those around you to step in with support. This isn't about waving a white flag; it's about waving a baton in a relay race, knowing when it's time to pass it on so you can catch your breath.

Identifying Your Needs: Guidance on Recognizing and Acknowledging Your Emotional and Practical Needs

First things first, let's get clear on what you actually need. This might sound straightforward, but often, we buzz through our busy lives like bees, barely pausing to consider what would really help us keep flying. Start by taking a moment to tune in to yourself. What's causing you stress? Is it the mountain of tasks at work, the back-to-back activities with your kids, or perhaps an emotional weight that's been tugging at your heart? Once you pinpoint the sources of your stress, you can start to identify what type of support would truly be beneficial. Maybe it's delegating some tasks, seeking emotional support, or just getting some time to yourself. Recognizing and acknowledging these needs is the first step in managing your well-being effectively.

Effective Communication Skills: How to Express Your Needs Clearly and Assertively Without Alienating Others

Now, how do you put these needs into words without coming off as needy or pushing people away? It's all in the approach. Communication is an art, especially when it involves asking for help. Use "I" statements to express your needs without blame or accusation. For example, saying "I feel overwhelmed by my workload and could use some help prioritizing," is clear and direct without being confrontational. Be as specific as possible—vagueness can lead to misunderstandings or inadequate support. And remember, timing is key. Choose a moment when the person you're talking to can give you their full attention, not when they're rushing out the door or in the middle of their own crisis.

Setting Expectations: The Importance of Setting Realistic Expectations When Asking for Support from Friends and Family

Setting realistic expectations is crucial when it comes to asking for support. It's about being honest with yourself and others about what's truly feasible. If you're asking a friend to help with childcare so you can manage work commitments, be clear about what this involves and ensure it's something they can reasonably accommodate. This clarity prevents resentment and disappointment and helps ensure that the support you receive truly alleviates your stress rather than adding to it.

Receiving Help Graciously: Tips for Accepting Help with Gratitude and Recognizing the Mutual Benefits of Support Within Relationships

Finally, accepting help graciously is as important as asking for it effectively. Recognize that offering support is a sign of care and respect and accept it with gratitude. Resist the urge to feel guilty or indebted—healthy relationships are built on mutual support and kindness. Instead, consider how accepting help not only benefits you but also strengthens the bonds of your relationships, creating a deeper sense of community and interconnectedness.

Navigating the delicate art of asking for and receiving support is not just about keeping your life running smoothly—it's about enriching your relationships and deepening your understanding of yourself and your needs. It's a testament to your strength and an invitation to those who care about you to contribute positively to your life. So next time you find yourself struggling under the weight of your responsibilities, remember that asking for help isn't a burden—it's an opportunity to let your relationships shine and to remind yourself that no one is meant to handle everything alone.

THE ROLE OF COMMUNITY IN PERSONAL GROWTH

Imagine a world where everyone around you cheers on your successes, lifts you when you're down, and genuinely cares about your growth—welcome to the power of community. In our individualistic societies, we often overlook the profound impact that a supportive community can have on our personal development. It's like having a personal cheerleading squad; but instead of pom-poms, they come equipped with empathy, shared experiences, and invaluable perspectives that can significantly boost your resilience and expand your horizons.

Finding Your Tribe: How to Find or Create a Community That Supports Your Interests, Values, and Self-Care Journey

Finding or creating your tribe might sound like a quest from a fantasy novel, but it's very much a real and rewarding venture. Start by identifying your values, passions and interests. As mentioned earlier, having common interests is a great way to build connections. When exploring common interest groups, pay attention to the vibe. Does it feel welcoming? Is there a sense of mutual respect and encouragement among members? Remember, the goal is not just to share interests but to foster a supportive environment that encourages personal and collective growth.

Creating your own community can also be incredibly fulfilling. Start small—invite a few acquaintances who share your interest for a casual meetup. Whether it's a book club, a cooking group, or a DIY crafts night, the key is consistency and openness. As your group meets regularly, the bonds will naturally strengthen, and the community will grow organically. Don't be afraid to set the tone by sharing your goals and encouraging others to share theirs. This can help establish a supportive atmosphere right from the start.

Community as a Support System: The Benefits of Having a Supportive Community for Personal Development and Resilience

A robust community acts as a fantastic buffer against life's inevitable stresses. Knowing you have a network of people who believe in you and are there to back you up can significantly lessen the blow of personal setbacks. Moreover, a community provides a diverse range of perspectives that can challenge and inspire you to think differently and grow. It's like having access to a collective brain—rich with different experiences and insights that can propel you forward in ways you might not manage on your own.

In times of crisis, this community becomes even more crucial. Whether it's a career hiccup, personal loss, or a global pandemic, having a network that offers emotional, and sometimes even physical, support can make all the difference. It's not just about having people to lean on; it's about feeling connected and valued, which are fundamental human needs. These connections foster resilience, making you more adept at navigating challenges and bouncing back quicker from setbacks.

Participating Actively: Ways to Engage with and Contribute to Your Community, Enhancing Both Personal Growth and Communal Well-Being

Engagement is the fuel that keeps the community engine running. By actively participating, you not only enrich your own life but also contribute to the vitality of the group. Volunteer for leadership roles or offer to organize events—these activities can help you develop new skills and gain confidence. Attending community events, workshops, and discussions also keeps the communal spirit vibrant and offers continual learning opportunities.

Moreover, active participation reinforces a sense of belonging and investment in the community's success. It's a reciprocal relationship; your growth contributes to the community's development, and the community's evolution fosters your personal growth. Sharing your skills and knowledge, whether through a formal presentation or a casual conversation, can also make a significant impact. It positions you as an active, contributing member and can be incredibly rewarding.

Virtual Communities: Leveraging Online Platforms to Connect with Like-Minded Individuals and Foster a Sense of Belonging

In today's digital age, virtual communities are as significant as physical ones. Online platforms can connect you with individuals from around the world who share your interests and values. These communities can be particularly valuable for those with niche interests or for those who live in remote areas where local communities may be limited. Platforms like forums, social media groups, and virtual workshops provide opportunities to engage and grow, all from the comfort of your home.

To make the most of these virtual spaces, actively participate in discussions, offer support to other members, and share your experiences and insights. The anonymity of online interactions can sometimes lead to a lack of accountability, so it's important to foster a respectful and supportive environment, much like you would in a physical community. Virtual connections can also lead to real-world friendships and opportunities, further enriching your community experience and expanding your support network beyond geographic boundaries.

Navigating the vibrant dynamics of community involvement offers a spectrum of benefits that enhance your personal growth, resilience, and sense of belonging. Whether through face-to-face interactions or virtual engagements, each connection, each shared experience, and each supportive exchange weaves a stronger, more supportive network that not only uplifts individuals but also strengthens the collective fabric of the community. As you continue to explore and engage with your communities, remember that each contribution, no matter how small, helps to build a more interconnected and supportive world.

LEVERAGING SOCIAL MEDIA FOR POSITIVE CONNECTIONS

Social media, oh the double-edged sword in our digital age! It can be a beacon of inspiration or a den of comparison, depending on how you wield it. Let's navigate these waters together, transforming your online experience into a source of joy rather than a stressor. The key lies in curating your feeds with the precision of a museum curator. This isn't about unfriending everyone who shares a picture of their exotic vacation or gourmet dinner. It's about consciously choosing whom and what to follow. Start by evaluating your current feed—do the posts you see uplift you or make you feel inadequate? Are you bombarded with negativity or inspired by positivity? Take control by following pages and people that share uplifting content, be it motivational quotes, educational content, or heartwarming stories. This digital diet will feed your mind with encouragement and genuine enjoyment, making your time spent on social media refreshing rather than draining.

Now, while curating helps in managing what you see, mindful usage is about managing how and when you engage with social media. It's tempting to scroll endlessly, but this habit often leads to more comparison and less connection. Set specific times for checking social media, and stick to them. Use apps if necessary to limit your time spent online. This disciplined approach helps prevent the mindless scroll that can eat into your time and affect your mental health. When you do log in, engage actively. Comment on posts that move you, share your thoughts, and interact with others. This active engagement makes your social media use more meaningful and rewarding, fostering connections rather than fostering envy.

Finding inspiration online is another fantastic way to harness the positive power of social media. Look for accounts that challenge you to grow, teach you new skills, or encourage you to pursue your passions. This could be a professional development coach, a health and wellness site, or artists and creatives who share their journeys. Engage with content that aligns with your interests and goals, and use these as stepping stones in your own personal and professional development. Remember, inspiration is a tool for growth, not a source of envy. Let the success and happiness of others inspire you to pursue your own, not diminish it.

The concept of a digital detox, while often touted, is truly beneficial. Just as your body needs a break from constant activity, your mind benefits from breaks from digital stimulation. Plan regular intervals—maybe a weekend or a certain day of the week—where you step back and disconnect. Use this time to reconnect with the offline world. Read a book, go for a walk, or spend time with loved ones. These breaks can refresh your perspective, making you more conscious of how and when you choose to engage online when you return.

ALONE BUT NOT LONELY: EMBRACING SOLITUDE

In a world that often confuses solitude with loneliness, there's a profound strength in discovering the joy of your own company. Solitude, far from being a sign of social deficiency, is a crucial ingredient for personal growth and self-discovery. It's the undisturbed silence that allows you to hear your thoughts more clearly and the peaceful isolation that can help you reconnect with your inner self. Embracing solitude isn't about shunning social interaction but about enriching your relationship with yourself, so you can engage more authentically with the world around you.

The Value of Solitude

Think of solitude as your personal retreat—an opportunity to step back from the social carousel and reflect on your journey, your choices, and your dreams. It's a space where you can explore your passions without distraction, where you can sort through your thoughts without external influence. This quiet introspection can lead to profound insights about your desires, your conflicts, and your place in the world. It's in these quiet moments that you often find the courage to make decisions that align more closely with your authentic self. Solitude is where you can recharge your emotional and mental batteries—essential for maintaining your overall well-being.

Solo Activities for Self-Reflection

If the idea of spending time alone seems daunting or you're unsure what to do, consider activities that foster introspection and self-understanding that have been highlighted for their positive impact on self-care earlier in this book:

- Journaling is a fantastic start. It's just you, a pen, and your thoughts, spilling onto paper without judgments or interruptions. Whether you're drafting a letter to your future self, sketching out your thoughts, or simply documenting your day, journaling can be a powerful tool for self-discovery and catharsis.
- Another enriching solo activity is meditation. Sitting quietly with your thoughts can help you develop greater mindfulness and reduce stress, enhancing your emotional clarity and peace of mind.
- If you're more of a nature lover, solo walks in a peaceful setting can be incredibly therapeutic. They combine the physical benefits of walking with the mental relief of being in nature, providing a double dose of self-care. Re-read the section earlier in this book on Forest Bathing for a quick refresher if needed (chapter 3.5).

Balancing Social Time and Alone Time

Finding the right balance between socializing and solitude can be tricky. It's like mixing the perfect cocktail—you need the right proportions to get it just right. Pay attention to how you feel after social interactions and periods of solitude. Do you feel drained or energized? Craving company or needing space? These emotional cues are your guide. If you're feeling overwhelmed by social engagements, it might be time to schedule a date with yourself. Conversely, if you're feeling isolated, it might be an indication to reach out to friends or family. Remember, balance is dynamic. As your life changes, your needs for social interaction and solitude will shift. Stay attuned to these changes and adjust your schedule accordingly to maintain a healthy balance that keeps you feeling rejuvenated and connected.

Embracing Being Single

For those who are single, embracing solitude can be particularly empowering. Being single offers a unique opportunity to build a relationship with yourself that is not influenced by a partner's needs or expectations. It's a time when you can explore your interests, invest in your personal growth, and define who you are on your own terms. Use this time to strengthen your self-sufficiency and to cultivate a lifestyle that brings you joy and fulfillment. Being single is not about waiting for someone to complete you; it's about using the time to grow into the best version of yourself, so when or if you choose to partner up, you're entering the relationship as a whole, fulfilled individual.

As we wrap up this chapter on social self-care and connection, we've navigated through the importance of friendships, the art of communication, the value of community, the influence of social media, and the power of solitude. Each section has offered insights into how to enrich your social interactions and personal growth. Remember, the quality of your relationships can significantly influence your happiness and well-being. As we move forward, let these insights guide you in nurturing connections that are supportive, enriching, and empowering. In the next chapter, we will explore the creative and spiritual dimensions of self-care, expanding our understanding of how these aspects can further enhance our journey towards a balanced and joyful life.

 Reflection Section – Learn Something New

"Learning is a treasure which will follow its owner everywhere."

CHINESE PROVERB

The value of learning is manifold, a theme we've consistently touched upon throughout this book. Let's briefly revisit the key advantages of embracing new knowledge:

- It fosters the creation of fresh neural connections in the brain.
- It bolsters self-assurance.
- It acts as a conduit for forming connections with individuals who share similar interests, thereby fulfilling our innate desire for companionship.
- It ignites creativity by introducing novel ideas and viewpoints,

With your journal in hand, find a blank page and begin to brainstorm all that you wish to learn. Allow your imagination free rein – the sky's the limit. Avoid being deterred by potential challenges at this juncture. Following that, proceed with these steps:

1. Highlight your top three learning desires.
2. Research the feasible ways to achieve them.
3. Devise a concrete plan and act on it.

Delight in the journey of discovery that learning brings.

CHAPTER 6 (DAYS 26 – 30)
THE CREATIVE AND SPIRITUAL DIMENSIONS OF SELF-CARE

I magine if your mind were a canvas, vast and blank, waiting for the vibrant colors of creativity and spirituality to bring it to life. In this chapter, we dive into the palette of your psyche, exploring how integrating creativity and curiosity into your daily life isn't just about making things; it's about making things better—your mood, your resilience, and, yes, even your health. Think of creativity not as a luxury but a vital nutrient for your soul, something as essential to your well-being as the air you breathe. Ready to color outside the lines? Let's unleash the power of your creative spirit and discover how it can transform stress into serenity and transform you into the best version of yourself.

CREATIVE OUTLETS FOR STRESS RELIEF

Exploring Creativity: The Benefits of Engaging in Creative Activities for Stress Reduction and Emotional Expression

Creativity is the playground of the mind, a place where the stresses of the adult world can be reshaped into something beautiful or at least manageable. Engaging in creative activities activates parts of your brain that can make you happier and more relaxed. It's like sending your brain on a mini-vacation, away from the worries of everyday life. Whether you're painting, writing, knitting, or dancing, these activities can serve as powerful antidotes to stress. They offer a form of expression that can be more potent than words, providing an outlet for emotions that might otherwise remain bottled up. Research suggests that creative expression can lower stress levels, improve mental health, and even enhance cognitive function as you age. So, whether you're doodling in a notebook, singing in a choir or redecorating your living room, know you're giving your brain a well-deserved break.

Finding Your Creative Medium: Tips for Discovering and Nurturing Your Creative Interests, Whether in Art, Writing, Music, or Crafts

Finding the creative medium that 'clicks' for you is like finding the perfect pair of jeans—satisfying and relieving. Start by revisiting the creative interests you had as a child. Did you enjoy drawing, singing, or making up stories? Sometimes, these early interests can provide clues to your natural inclinations. If you're starting from scratch, give yourself permission to experiment. Sign up for a pottery class, try your hand at poetry, or learn an instrument. The key is approaching this exploration with curiosity and playfulness— no pressure to produce a masterpiece. Remember, this is about the process, not just the product. As you try different activities, notice which ones make you lose track of time, which feel like joyful exploration, and which leave you feeling proud and energized. These are your clues, leading you to the creative path that suits you best.

Creative Rituals for Everyday Life: Incorporating Small Creative Practices into Your Daily Routine for Ongoing Stress Management

Incorporating creativity into your daily life doesn't require grand gestures or hours of free time. It's about weaving small, creative practices into your routine. Start with something simple, like keeping a sketchbook on your coffee table for impromptu doodling or setting aside ten minutes each morning to write in a journal. You could create a playlist to inspire you during mundane tasks like cooking or cleaning or take a different route to snap photos of interesting sights on your walk to work. These small acts of creativity can be mini-escapes throughout your day, refreshing your mind and boosting your mood. Make these practices as habitual as your morning coffee; let them be the moments of delight and surprise that punctuate your everyday routine.

Overcoming Creative Blocks: Strategies for Moving Past Fears and Blocks That Hinder Your Creative Expression

Creative blocks, much like traffic jams, are frustrating and, at times, seemingly inexplicable. But they're also a natural part of the creative process. The first step in overcoming these blocks is recognizing and accepting them without judgment. Treat yourself with the kindness you would offer a friend in a similar situation. Next, try changing your environment. A change of scenery can stimulate new ideas and perspectives. If you're stuck indoors, even rearranging your furniture or decluttering can shift your mental state. If fear of imperfection is holding you back, permit yourself to make 'bad art.' The goal is expression, not perfection. Sometimes, simply starting—no matter how messy or imperfect—can break the dam of creative stagnation. Remember, every artist, writer, and creator has faced this challenge. You're in good company; like them, you'll find your flow again.

Interactive   Element: Journaling Prompt

To further explore and unlock your creative potential, here's a journaling prompt: Write about a time when you felt most creative— even if it was when you were a child. What were you doing? How did it make you feel? Reflecting on this can reignite your passion and provide clues to your natural creative preferences, guiding you back to activities that light up your imagination and spirit.

As we paint our way through this chapter, remember that creativity isn't just about producing art—it's about crafting a life that feels like art. It's about viewing the world with wonder and curiosity and finding joy in creation. So, grab your metaphorical paintbrush, and let's color your world with the hues of imagination and innovation.

INCORPORATING NATURE INTO YOUR SPIRITUAL PRACTICE

Previously, we considered the healing power of nature, and in particular, the impact of outdoor activities, such as forest bathing, on our well-being. Now, let's consider nature and its potential impact on our spiritual practice. There's something undeniably spiritual about immersing yourself in the natural world. It reconnects us to the earth, reminds us of the cycle of life, and provides a profound sense of peace and grounding. In its unbounded glory, nature serves not just as a backdrop for our lives but as an active participant in our spiritual well-being.

Nature as a Spiritual Sanctuary

In today's fast-paced digital world, stepping into nature allows us to disconnect from technological tethers and reconnect with ourselves and the universe. It's about finding a quiet spot where the only sounds are the wind, water, and wildlife. Here, amidst the simplicity of nature, you can find clarity and peace. With its intricate beauty and inherent wisdom, the natural world provides a perfect setting for reflection and spiritual connection. Whether it's a forest, a beach, or your backyard, nature has a way of stripping away the superficial, revealing what truly matters in life.

Creating a personal sanctuary in nature doesn't require vast expanses of wilderness; even a small garden or a local park can serve as your spiritual retreat. Engage with the environment mindfully. Notice the patterns of the leaves, the play of light and shadow, and the myriad hues of green. Let nature's peace seep into your soul, calming your mind and enriching your spirit. This connection can help deepen your understanding of your place in the cosmos, fostering a sense of belonging to something greater than yourself.

Mindful Nature Walks: Techniques for Cultivating Mindfulness and Presence During Time Spent Outdoors

Mindful walking in nature can transform a simple stroll into a profound spiritual practice. It's about walking not just with your feet but with your senses fully engaged. Begin by leaving behind your digital devices to ensure your attention isn't divided. As you walk, focus on your breath, feeling the air enter and leave your body, anchoring you to the present moment. With each step, feel the connection between your feet and the earth. Observe everything around you with a sense of curiosity and wonder. Each step is an opportunity to cultivate gratitude for the earth's abundant beauty and a chance to harmonize your inner rhythm with the natural world around you.

This practice enhances your physical presence and deepens your spiritual connection to the environment. It's a meditation in motion, where each step leads you deeper into mindfulness. The rhythmic pattern of walking helps to quiet the mind, making it receptive to the subtle spiritual energies of nature. This connection can lead to profound insights and a renewed sense of peace that you carry with you long after your walk ends.

Eco-Spirituality Practices: Ideas for Integrating Environmental Consciousness into Spiritual Practices

Eco-spirituality bridges the gap between spiritual practice and environmental consciousness, recognizing the sacredness of all life and our responsibility to protect it. It's about seeing the divine in all life forms and acting to preserve that divinity. One simple way to practice eco-spirituality is through ritual. For instance, you might create a small altar in your garden or home with natural elements, such as stones, plants, and water. This altar can serve as a focal point for meditation and reflection, reminding you of your connection to the earth and your role in its stewardship.

Another practice is participating in clean-up activities in your local environment, whether a beach, park, or woodland. These actions can be meditative and deeply spiritual. They are acts of care for the planet that reflect your spiritual values and foster a tangible connection to the earth. You might also consider adopting sustainable practices in your daily life, such as reducing waste, conserving water, or supporting eco-friendly businesses. These actions, rooted in spiritual commitment, can help you live in harmony with nature, making every day an expression of your eco-spiritual values.

The Healing Power of Plants: Engaging with Plant Care and Gardening as Forms of Spiritual and Self-Care Practices

Gardening and plant care are deeply meditative and nurturing practices that can enhance your spiritual life. There's a healing power in tending to plants, nurturing life, and watching it flourish. This connection to the cycle of life and growth can be incredibly grounding and uplifting. Start by choosing plants that resonate with you, whether for their beauty, fragrance, or the peace they instill. As you water, prune, and care for them, do so with mindfulness and intention. Think of each act of care as a prayer or meditation.

This practice not only brings you closer to nature but also to your own spiritual essence. It teaches patience, care, and the beauty of growth—both in the plants you nurture and in yourself. The lessons plants teach us—about resilience, blooming at our own pace, and the impact of nurturing attention—are metaphors for our spiritual journeys. Engaging regularly with plants can make your home a living sanctuary, a space imbued with life, and a constant reminder of your connection to the natural world.

THE BASICS OF CURIOSITY: INTRODUCING THE BENEFITS OF BEING CURIOUS

Curiosity extends beyond seeking answers; it embodies a zeal for continuous learning, exploration, and personal evolution. This innate passion serves as the catalyst that ignites our imagination, paving the way for discovery, comprehension, fresh viewpoints, and novel experiences. Acting as vital drivers for uncovering one's purpose and chasing after one's passions, curiosity, and commitment to lifelong learning are indispensable. They are the core attributes that propel us toward exploration, innovation, and self-improvement. These traits urge us to adopt an open-minded stance, embrace adventure, and nurture an enthusiasm for the world around us, culminating in a life that is both enriching and purposeful.

Embracing curiosity allows us to perceive the world through a different lens, engaging our observational skills to their fullest extent. This state of heightened engagement and vitality empowers us to seize opportunities, forge meaningful connections, and experience profound moments of insight and significance. These experiences lay the groundwork for a life characterized by richness, awareness, and profound satisfaction.

The Relationship Between Curiosity and Self-Care

Curiosity is a cornerstone in a woman's self-care journey, fostering a spirit of discovery and an unending quest for learning that are crucial for profound personal growth and holistic well-being. This insatiable thirst for knowledge encourages her to seek new information on wellness, engage with various self-care methodologies, and customize practices that align perfectly with her unique life circumstances. By actively pursuing a deeper understanding of self-care, she broadens her horizons and strengthens her resolve and resilience. This journey of exploration ensures that her self-care routine is not only personalized but also profoundly transformative, leading to practices that deeply resonate and have a lasting impact on her life.

FINDING YOUR FLOW: THE PSYCHOLOGY OF ENGAGEMENT WITH ACTIVITIES

Have you ever been so immersed in an activity that the world around you seemed to disappear? Where hours felt like minutes, and you emerged feeling energized and fulfilled? That, my friend, is the magic of the flow state, a concept developed by psychologist Mihaly Csikszentmihalyi. It's like being in the zone, but not just any zone—this is the ultimate performance sweet spot where you're fully engaged, your skills are utilized to their fullest, and you're producing your best work. Imagine you're a jazz musician, lost in a complex improvisation; each note flows effortlessly from your fingers, and you're not just playing music but living it. This state isn't reserved for artists or athletes alone; it's accessible to anyone, whether you're writing a report, gardening, or even solving a challenging puzzle.

Understanding Flow State

Flow is characterized by complete absorption in what one does, resulting in a loss of one's sense of space and time. It's like the world has narrowed to the task at hand, and you're laser-focused; everything else disappears. This intense concentration is not a byproduct of forcing yourself to focus. Still, it comes naturally when you're engaged in something challenging yet enjoyable. The beauty of flow is that it's also associated with a spike in dopamine, that feel-good neurotransmitter that helps elevate your mood and enhance your overall well-being. So, not only are you achieving great things, but you're also feeling fantastic while doing it.

Activities That Promote Flow

Identifying activities that can trigger this state is deeply personal. It often involves tasks that challenge you but don't overwhelm you, aligning neatly with your skills. For you, it might be writing, where words pour out like water, or perhaps it's strategic games that make your mind perform mental gymnastics. Others might find their flow in physical activities like yoga, where the combination of movement and breath creates a rhythmic dance that captivates their entire being. To discover your flow activities, reflect on past experiences where you've lost track of time. What were you doing? How can you incorporate more of that into your routine? Remember, the goal here isn't just to keep busy but to engage deeply.

The Benefits of Flow for Self-Care

Incorporating flow activities into your life can dramatically boost your mental health. Regularly entering flow can reduce anxiety, combat depression, and increase your overall life satisfaction. When you're in flow, petty worries and stressors melt away, giving your mind a much-needed break from the usual chatter and worries. This isn't just a temporary reprieve; regularly engaging in flow activities can help you develop a more resilient, happier baseline state over time. It's akin to equipping your mental toolkit with the ultimate stress-relief weapon that enables you to cope with stress and enriches your life in the process.

Cultivating Conditions for Flow

Creating the right environment and mindset for flow involves a bit of setup but is well worth the effort. Start by choosing the right time —when are you most alert and free from interruptions? For many, this might be early morning or late at night when the world is quiet. Next, tailor your environment to reduce distractions. This might mean clearing clutter from your workspace, putting your phone on do not disturb, or even investing in noise-canceling headphones. Setting clear goals and having all your tools at hand before you start can also help you slip into flow more easily. The key is preparation; reducing friction points allows you to dive deeper into the task with less effort.

As you explore and engage with activities that foster your flow state, remember that this is not about pushing yourself into burnout. It's about finding joy and satisfaction in the challenges that make you stretch but not snap. This delicate balance makes flow so deeply satisfying and why it can be a powerful component of your self-care regimen. So, go ahead, find your flow, and let it lift you to heights of creativity and fulfillment that make every day a little brighter, bolder, and much more enjoyable.

THE ART OF VISUALIZATION AND MANIFESTATION

Imagine if you could paint your future with the brush of your mind, coloring your life with the hues of your deepest desires and wildest dreams. This is the essence of visualization—a powerful, almost magical process where you picture your ideal future and, in doing so, bring it into your reality. Think of it as your mind's eye crafting a blueprint of your future successes, a mental rehearsal that prepares you for the real performance. Visualization isn't just wishful thinking; it's a deliberate, focused activity that harnesses the power of your subconscious to influence your behavior and mindset, aligning them with your goals.

Principles of Visualization

The principle behind visualization is simple yet profound: what you focus on expands. By vividly picturing yourself achieving your goals, you stimulate the same neural networks that would fire if you were actually performing the activity, enhancing your motivation and reinforcing your belief in your ability to succeed. It's like creating a mental muscle memory, priming your brain and body to act in ways that support your aspirations. For instance, an athlete might visualize winning a race, experiencing not just the sight of crossing the finish line but the sounds of the crowd, the feel of the track underfoot, and the swell of pride. This vivid mental imagery can improve focus, boost confidence, and enhance performance by preparing the mind and body for action.

Manifestation Techniques

While visualization sets the stage, manifestation is where you bring the curtain up on your performance. Manifestation takes visualization a step further, aligning your thoughts, actions, and energy with your desired outcome. It's like planting and nurturing a seed with the right soil, water, and sunlight. Start with clarity—be clear about what you want to achieve. Ambiguity can send mixed signals to your brain, diluting the effectiveness of your efforts. Next, infuse your goal with positive energy. Approach it with hope and enthusiasm, not desperation or fear. This positive mindset attracts opportunities and opens doors that align with your aspirations.

A powerful manifestation technique is affirming your intentions. Use positive affirmations that reinforce your goals, such as "I am capable of achieving great things" or "I attract abundance into my life." Repeat these daily, and act as if your affirmation is already true. This boosts your confidence and aligns your actions with your goals. Additionally, creating a vision board can serve as a daily visual reminder of your aspirations, keeping your attention focused on your objectives and maintaining your motivational momentum.

Overcoming Limiting Beliefs

Often, the biggest hurdles in visualization and manifestation are the limiting beliefs that reside in our own minds. These nagging doubts and negative assumptions about our abilities or worthiness can sabotage our success. Identifying these beliefs is the first step to dismantling them. Reflect on thoughts that arise when you consider your goals. Do you think things like "I'm not good enough" or "It's too late for me"? Challenge these beliefs by asking yourself whether they are indeed accurate, what evidence supports or contradicts them, and how they might hold you back.

Once you've identified a limiting belief, work on rewriting it. Transform "I'm not good enough" into "I am worthy and capable." This isn't about denying your feelings but about reshaping your perspective to empower rather than limit you. Regularly practicing this shift in mindset can gradually change your internal narrative, enhancing your self-esteem and opening you up to pursue your goals with confidence and clarity.

Daily Practices for Manifestation

To make visualization and manifestation part of your daily routine:

1. Integrate simple practices that reinforce your focus and intention.
2. Begin each day by visualizing your ideal day or a specific goal as vividly as possible.
3. Spend a few minutes in meditation, focusing on your intentions for the day.
4. Carry a small object, like a stone or a piece of jewelry, that reminds you of your goals, touching it throughout the day to center your focus.
5. Before bed, reflect on the actions you took that day that moved you closer to your goals, however small, and visualize taking the next steps.

These practices help keep your goals at the forefront of your mind, continuously aligning your thoughts and actions with your desires. They turn every day into a step towards realizing your dreams, making each day purposeful and focused. Visualization and manifestation are not just about achieving external goals; they are transformative practices that can enhance your self-awareness, boost your confidence, and enrich your journey toward personal fulfillment.

As we close this chapter on visualization and manifestation, remember that the power to shape your future lies within you. Your mind is a powerful tool, capable of influencing your reality in profound ways. By mastering the arts of visualization and manifestation, you equip yourself with the skills to dream of your ideal future and actively bring it into being. Let these practices be your guide as you paint the canvas of your life with the vibrant colors of your hopes, dreams, and aspirations. Now, let's turn the page to explore the next chapter, where we will delve into overcoming challenges to self-care, ensuring that you are equipped to maintain your well-being even in the face of life's inevitable ups and downs.

 Reflection Section – Curiosity Corner

"Curiosity is one of the great secrets of happiness."

BRYANT MCGILL

Which dimension of self-care has captured your attention and curiosity? Do you find yourself drawn to deepening your knowledge in nutrition, eager to understand the intricate science of happiness hormones, fascinated by the principles of positive psychology, inclined towards the calming practices of meditation and mindfulness, or experimenting with the power of manifestation and visualisation?

Pause and ponder the various topics we've explored in this self-care odyssey. In your journal, pinpoint the sphere you're most passionate about investigating further. Note down any burning questions or areas of uncertainty you may have. Commit to allocating time for research, aiming to peel back layers of complexity and gain a richer, more nuanced understanding. This deliberate quest for knowledge will broaden your perspective and significantly enhance your self-care practice with insights uniquely tailored to your journey.

CHAPTER 7
OVERCOMING CHALLENGES TO SELF-CARE

I magine you've decided to plant a garden. You've lovingly selected the seeds, plotted the soil, and looked forward to bountiful blooms. But then, life happens. A surprise frost, an unexpected downpour, or maybe the seeds just don't sprout despite your best efforts. In gardening, as in self-care, what do you do? You adapt, learn, and sometimes start afresh with a new batch of seeds or a different strategy. Adapting isn't just about survival; it's about thriving and finding new ways to blossom even when conditions change.

REVISITING AND REVISING GOALS: THE PIVOT PRINCIPLE

Flexibility in Goal Setting

Flexibility might sound like the yoga class you've been meaning to try but haven't yet (and that's okay!), but here, it's about keeping your self-care goals adaptable. Your self-care needs will shift as your life evolves—new job, new relationships, new challenges. What worked for you last year might not fit anymore, and that's not just okay; it's expected. Think of your self-care routine as a bespoke suit. Occasionally, it needs tailoring to fit the current you, not the you from five years ago. This means being honest about what is and isn't working. It's about giving yourself permission to change your mind, to swap out meditation in the quiet dawn for a dance class that makes your heart sing and your body sweat. It's about making your self-care fit your life, not squeezing your life to fit into your self-care.

The Pivot Principle

Now, pivoting isn't just for basketball players or tech startups. It's a vital skill in the art of self-care. Recognizing when it's time to pivot comes from staying connected to how you feel about your routines. Are they still bringing you peace and joy, or have they become another checkbox on your crowded to-do list? When you notice that something feels off, that's your cue to pivot. This doesn't mean overhauling your entire life; sometimes, the smallest adjustments make the biggest difference. Maybe it's shifting your workout times, trying a new nutrition plan, or finding creative ways to connect with friends. Listen to your life; it has a way of whispering what needs to change before it starts to scream.

Continuous Assessment

Keeping a regular check on your self-care routines isn't much different from a regular check-up at the doctor. It's preventive care for your lifestyle. This might mean setting a monthly reminder to review your activities, feelings, and overall satisfaction with your self-care practices. Ask yourself, "Is this still serving me? What do I need more or less of?" This regular audit ensures that your self-care regimen remains dynamic and responsive to your needs, preventing it from becoming stale or ineffective.

Embracing Change

Change is often seen as the big, scary monster under the bed. But what if we flipped the narrative? What if change is the ticket to your next big adventure in self-care? Embracing change means seeing each twist and turn in your life as an opportunity to grow and learn. It means not clinging too tightly to "how things have always been" and being open to exploration and experimentation. After all, self-care should be a lively dance, not a rigid march. When you embrace change, you open yourself up to new possibilities, new joys, and new ways that might be better than the old ones.

Interactive Element: Journal Prompt

Take a moment now to reflect on your current self-care goals. Grab your journal and jot down what's working and what isn't. How have your life circumstances changed since you first set these goals? Are there goals that feel more like burdens now? What small pivot could you make today to realign these goals with your current lifestyle and desires? Remember, this isn't about criticism but curiosity and care.

DEALING WITH SELF-CARE FATIGUE: SIGNS AND SOLUTIONS

Imagine hitting that snooze button on your alarm, not because you need more sleep, but because the thought of your morning yoga routine suddenly feels as appealing as a cold shower in winter. Or perhaps the salad you used to whip up with enthusiasm now seems as dreary as doing your taxes. These could be signs that your self-care routine isn't caring for you right now. Yes, self-care can become a chore, another box to tick off in your already crammed to-do list, leading to what I like to call 'self-care fatigue.' Recognizing this isn't just about admitting a temporary defeat; it's about tuning in to what your mind and body are asking for.

Self-care fatigue creeps in quietly. It starts with a slight reluctance towards your routines and can evolve into a complete aversion. You might notice feelings of irritability just thinking about your self-care activities, or perhaps you experience guilt for not enjoying or wanting to engage in practices that are supposed to make you feel better. Recognizing these feelings is the first step toward addressing self-care fatigue. It's like realizing that the cozy blanket you loved in winter is now just making you sweat in the summer. It served you well, but it's time for a change.

Now, let's talk about variety and moderation. Ever heard the saying, "Too much of a good thing can be wonderful"? Well, that wasn't about self-care routines. Doing the same activities day in and day out can dull their impact, making what was once refreshing feel mind-numbingly repetitive. Injecting variety into your self-care can reinvigorate your interest and enhance its benefits. It's like adding a splash of vibrant color to a fading painting. One day, you could be journaling; the next, you might find solace in a long walk or perhaps try out a new recipe that tickles your taste buds and nourishes your soul. The key is to keep it fresh, exciting, and, most importantly, fun.

And then there's the permission to rest. Yes, you heard that right. Resting is a form of self-care, too. Sometimes, the best thing you can do for yourself is nothing at all. This isn't about being lazy; it's about listening to what your body and mind need. It's okay to put your self-care routine on pause. Use this time to reflect, or better yet, don't use it at all. Let your mind wander, binge-watch that series, or stare at the ceiling if that feels right. Rest can help reset your mental state, making you more productive and enthusiastic about self-care when you resume.

Rekindling your self-care passion can sometimes feel like trying to start a fire with wet wood. It's frustrating, but with the right techniques, it's definitely doable. Start small. It's not about overhauling your entire routine but reigniting that spark with small, enjoyable activities. Maybe it's buying a new plant, joining a dance class, or simply taking a different route on your walk. You could also try combining self-care with social activities. How about a spa day with friends or a cooking night with family? Sometimes, sharing these moments with others can remind you why you started them in the first place. Remember, self-care isn't just about solitary activities; it's about creating joy and connections, which can sometimes mean inviting others into your self-care space.

By acknowledging the signs of self-care fatigue and allowing yourself the flexibility to adapt, rest, and inject fun and variety into your routines, you can ensure that self-care remains a joyous and beneficial part of your life, not just another task on your checklist. Remember, self-care is supposed to be your lifeline, not your chore. Treat it as a treasure chest full of exciting possibilities and watch it transform your life, one joyful moment at a time.

WHEN LIFE GETS IN THE WAY: ADJUSTING YOUR SELF-CARE PLAN

Imagine you're following a delicious recipe for a lemon meringue pie. You've got your ingredients lined up, in your apron, and ready to whip up a storm. But then, the oven breaks. What do you do? Scrap the whole dessert? No way! Maybe you can adapt and make a no-bake cheesecake instead. Similarly, your self-care routine must be flexible enough to adapt when life's proverbial ovens break down. Life doesn't just throw lemons; sometimes, it hurls the whole tree. Adapting isn't about giving up on self-care; it's about tweaking it to fit the new mold life casts for you.

Adapting to life's demands means acknowledging that your self-care routine isn't set in stone. It's a living, breathing plan that should morph as your life does. Got a new job that demands early mornings? It might be time to shift your meditative morning run to a calming evening walk. Just had a baby? Your hour-long yoga session might need to transform into bite-sized stretches throughout the day. The key here is to maintain the essence of your self-care activities, even if their format needs to change. It's about preserving the spirit, if not the letter, of your self-care law. This adaptability ensures that self-care remains a relief, not a chore added to your ever-growing list of tasks.

Now, distinguishing between short-term and long-term adjustments is crucial. Short-term tweaks might include skipping a few workout sessions during a particularly hectic week or substituting meditation with deep-breathing exercises when time is sparse. These are akin to taking a detour but still aiming to reach the same destination. On the other hand, long-term changes are more about changing the destination itself. These might be necessary when you experience significant life changes, like moving to a new city or undergoing a major career shift. Your entire self-care routine might need an overhaul to better suit your new circumstances. It's about re-evaluating your needs, and resources and finding new ways to meet them, whilst of course keeping your values in mind.

In navigating through the unpredictability of life, remember that your self-care routine shouldn't be another source of stress but a flexible framework that helps you handle stress. It's your secret ingredient to surviving and thriving, no matter what life decides to cook up.

OVERCOMING FINANCIAL BARRIERS TO SELF-CARE

Let's face it, the phrase 'self-care' often conjures images of luxurious spa days, exotic retreats, and pricey wellness products— enough to make your wallet break into a cold sweat. But here's a refreshing twist: self-care doesn't have to dent your bank account. It's entirely possible to pamper your body, mind, and soul on a shoestring budget or even for free! The essence of self-care is about feeling good and taking good care of yourself, and that certainly doesn't require a luxury tag. So, let's roll up our sleeves (figuratively, of course, because this is about relaxation) and delve into how you can sustain your well-being without stretching your finances.

Affordable self-care is about simplicity and creativity—think less about buying your way to relaxation and more about tuning into what truly rejuvenates you without a price tag. Start with the basics: sleep, nutrition, hydration, and physical activity. These are the pillars of health and surprisingly fall into the category of low-cost self-care. Prioritize a good night's sleep by establishing a calming bedtime routine—think soothing music and avoiding screens, rather than purchasing luxury bedding. Regarding nutrition, simple home-cooked meals often trump expensive health food products. Beans, rice, seasonal vegetables, and fruits can be the superheroes of your kitchen, nourishing your body without draining your wallet.

Physical activity is another arena where you can dodge high costs with ease. Swap the gym membership for home workouts or community yoga sessions in the park. Even better, take a walk or jog outside; nature offers a free venue and the added bonus of fresh air. The internet is bursting with free resources—from workout videos to meditation guides—that can bolster your self-care routine at no additional cost. Libraries also offer a treasure trove of wellness books and relaxation CDs you can borrow instead of buy.

Now, let's talk about prioritizing spending because managing finances is, frankly, a crucial part of self-care. It begins with evaluating what aspects of your current self-care routine are truly worth investing in and what can be modified for a more budget-friendly version. This could mean choosing which products or services provide you the most value and setting aside a specific portion of your budget for these. It's about making informed choices—opting for a quality pair of running shoes if you're into jogging, for instance, while foregoing fancy juice cleanses.

Community resources are an under-tapped reservoir of self-care opportunities. Many communities offer free or low-cost fitness classes, mental health workshops, and other wellness-oriented activities. Local health fairs often provide free screenings, vaccinations, and valuable health information. Community gardens invite you to connect with nature and your neighbors while getting your hands dirty—a therapeutic activity and a source of fresh produce. Also, consider reaching out to community centers, local non-profits, or faith-based organizations; they often have resources or events that focus on improving mental and physical health.

By embracing these strategies, you can ensure that your journey toward maintaining health and happiness is effective and economical. Self-care is inherently personal, and with creativity and resourcefulness, it can be an enriching part of your life, free from financial worries. So next time you think about self-care, remember that it's not about the money you spend; it's about the moments you invest in yourself.

FINDING MOTIVATION: WHAT TO DO WHEN YOU'RE STUCK

Sometimes, when it comes to self-care, the hardest part isn't starting—it's keeping going, especially on days when your sofa seems like a much better friend than your yoga mat. It's like trying to push a stalled car; no matter how much you know you should move, the motivation isn't there. So, what's the secret to getting unstuck? It begins with revisiting your 'why.'

Reflecting on why you started your self-care regimen, and the values you highlighted, can act like a mental defibrillator, shocking your motivation back to life. Remember the initial reasons that nudged you towards self-care. Was it to feel healthier? To manage stress better? Or perhaps to carve out some 'me' time in your bustling life? Reconnecting with these reasons can reignite your motivation because it reminds you of the value these practices add to your life. It's not just about the activities themselves but the benefits they bring—more energy, less stress, a greater sense of peace. Sometimes, writing these reasons down or creating a vision board can help keep them fresh in your mind, serving as a daily reminder of why you're doing what you're doing.

Next, let's review what we know about setting small, achievable goals. When motivation is low, even small tasks can seem daunting. Break down your self-care into bite-sized pieces. Instead of an hour-long workout, aim for a quick 15-minute walk. Instead of a full weekend of meal prepping, try preparing just one healthy meal. These small victories can be incredibly powerful, building momentum and a sense of accomplishment. Each small goal achieved is a step in the right direction, slowly but surely rekindling your motivation. It's about celebrating the little wins; knowing each brings you closer to the larger picture of well-being.

Celebrating progress, no matter how small, is crucial. Every step forward is worth acknowledgment. Did you choose a salad over fast food? Give yourself a pat on the back. Did you manage to meditate for five minutes today? That's another win. These celebrations can boost your morale and remind you that progress, not perfection, is the goal. Keeping a journal of your successes or setting up a reward system for meeting small milestones can enhance this effect, making the journey enjoyable and rewarding.

You can pull yourself out of the motivation mire by weaving these strategies into your life. It's about understanding and harnessing what drives you, celebrating small successes, and leaning on the support of a community. With these tools, you're not just pushing that stalled car anymore—you're firing up the engine and ready to roll.

As we wrap up this chapter on overcoming challenges to self-care, remember that every journey has its bumps and detours. The key is not to get caught up in the obstacles but to focus on the strategies that help navigate them. Whether it's pivoting your goals, injecting variety into your routines, adjusting to life's demands, finding budget-friendly ways to care for yourself, or steering through major life transitions, each challenge offers growth and renewal opportunities. Keep your motivation toolkit handy, and remember that with the right mindset and strategies, you can keep your self-care journey on track, no matter what life throws your way.

Next, we move into sustaining these self-care practices in the long term. It's about turning your learning into lifelong habits that support and nourish you daily. Let's continue to build a foundation that keeps you strong, resilient, and thriving.

Reflection Section: Self-Care Check-In

Take a few moments to consider the Self-Care Check-In below and ask yourself these questions:

- ☐ Are you doing these things?
- ☐ Where do I feel I am being successful with my self-care habits?
- ☐ Which element of your self-care practices needs some more attention?
- ☐ Are there any self-care practices you would like to do differently?

- **Hydration**: Do I drink at least 8 glasses of water daily?
- **Nutrition**: Are my meals balanced with fruits, vegetables, proteins, and grains?
- **Exercise**: Do I engage in physical activity regularly?
- **Sleep**: Am I getting 7-9 hours of quality sleep each night?
- **Mindfulness**: Do I practice meditation and / or deep breathing?
- **Nature**: Do I spend time outdoors?
- **Screen Time**: Do I limit my use of digital devices?
- **Relationships**: Do I nurture my relationships with family and friends?
- **Hobbies**: Do I make time for activities I enjoy?
- **Organization**: Is my living and work space tidy?
- **Health Check-Ups**: Do I schedule regular health screenings?
- **Gratitude**: Do I practice gratitude daily?

- **Boundaries**: Am I setting and respecting personal boundaries?
- **Learning**: Am I continuously learning something new?
- **Self-Care**: Do I pamper myself regularly?
- **Affirmations**: Do I use positive affirmations daily?
- **Visualization**: Do I visualize my goals and dreams?
- **Stress Management**: Do I have effective strategies for managing stress?
- **Personal Growth**: Am I working towards personal growth and self-improvement?
- **Relaxation**: Do I take time to relax and unwind daily?

This checklist can help you review and enhance your self-care practices.

This chapter emphasizes the importance of adopting a flexible, growth-centric approach to self-care practices, transforming them from routine activities into dynamic and enriching aspects of your existence that mature and expand with one.

CULTIVATING A GROWTH MINDSET FOR CONTINUOUS SELF-IMPROVEMENT

Growth Mindset Foundations: Introducing the concept of a growth mindset and its role in continuous self-improvement.

A term coined by psychologist Carol Dweck, a growth mindset refers to the belief that your abilities and intelligence can be developed over time through dedication and hard work. This is the antithesis of a fixed mindset, which suggests that our abilities are static and unchangeable. But how does this relate to self-care? Integrating a growth mindset into your self-care practices means embracing challenges, persisting in the face of setbacks, and understanding that each step—no matter how small—is a progression towards a healthier, happier you. It's about celebrating the effort, not just the outcome. Whether trying a new yoga pose and toppling over or meditating for the first time and finding your mind wandering to your grocery list—it's all part of the process. Each effort enriches your understanding of what your body and mind need.

Challenges as Opportunities: Viewing challenges as opportunities for growth rather than obstacles

In the realm of self-care, challenges are not roadblocks; they are stepping stones to deeper self-understanding and resilience. Missed a week of workouts? Each day is a new opportunity to understand what barriers exist and how to navigate them. Struggling to sleep well? Each restless night is a chance to tweak your bedtime routine, leading you closer to those coveted zzz's. It's about flipping the script from frustration to curiosity—what can this challenge teach me about my needs and preferences?

Lifelong Learning: Encouraging an attitude of lifelong learning and curiosity as part of self-care

Self-care is not a finite goal; it's a continuous journey of discovery. Lifelong learning in the context of self-care involves:

- Staying curious about emerging wellness trends.
- Understanding the evolving needs of your body and mind.
- Continuously adapting your practices as you age.

It's about reading the latest book on mindfulness, attending workshops, or even listening to podcasts about holistic health. This commitment to learning keeps your practices fresh and effective, ensuring they grow as you do.

Embracing Failure: How to embrace failure as a step towards growth and not a reflection of self-worth

Failure, in the world of self-care, is a misnomer. Every misstep is a valuable feedback loop, not a setback. Didn't stick to your diet plan? Rather than wallowing in self-criticism, assess what went awry. Perhaps the plan was too rigid, or life just happened—birthday parties, office treats, or simply the lure of your favorite comfort food. Each "failure" is a clue to what can be improved, adjusted, or transformed to better suit your real-life scenarios. Embracing these moments without judgment allows you to tweak your approach, ensuring your self-care regimen is realistic, flexible, and forgiving— much like you should be towards yourself.

Nurturing this garden of self-care with a growth mindset cultivates better health and well-being; it also grows a more resilient, adaptable, and compassionate self. So, as you turn each page, consider it an invitation to plant new seeds of wellness, water them with curiosity and resilience, and watch as your garden of self-care flourishes into something uniquely beautiful and enduring.

THE ROLE OF RESILIENCE IN SELF-CARE

Imagine resilience as that trusty old umbrella you whip out when the skies decide to open up unexpectedly. It's not about avoiding the rain but walking through it without getting soaked. Building resilience through self-care is akin to fortifying your personal umbrella with the sturdiest of materials, ensuring you can weather any storm life throws your way, be it a drizzle or a deluge. Resilience isn't born only out of monumental struggles; it's crafted daily through the quiet, consistent practices of self-care that keep your spirits buoyed and your resolve strong.

Strategies for building resilience can seem as varied as the patterns on raincoats at a fashion show, but they often share common threads. Firstly, consider resilience-building as a daily workout for your emotional muscles. Just as you wouldn't run a marathon without training, you can't expect to handle life's marathons without prepping your mind. Engaging in regular mindfulness practices, such as meditation or deep-breathing exercises, strengthens your mental fortitude, allowing you to remain centered during crises. Regular physical activity also plays a crucial role. It's not just about sculpting those biceps or getting heart-healthy; it's about carving out time to disconnect from the chaos and reconnect with yourself, releasing those feel-good endorphins that act as natural stress buffers.

Then there's the power of connection, which, in the realm of resilience, works much like a shared umbrella in a downpour. We already know that cultivating strong, supportive relationships provides emotional shelter when the going gets tough. Its worth re-iterating that knowing you have people who have your back, who you can laugh with, cry with, or binge-watch your favorite shows with on a tough day can make all the difference. These connections often provide the strength and perspective to bounce back from life's challenges.

Resilience is also deeply intertwined with emotional well-being. It's not just about bouncing back; it's about growing through what you go through. This growth is often visible in the way you handle emotional upheavals. With resilience, a setback is less likely to derail you for long. Instead, you can process your emotions more healthily and effectively, whether by seeking professional help, engaging in reflective practices like journaling, (as explored in detail earlier in this guide), or simply allowing time to grieve and heal. Recognizing that it's okay to not be okay sometimes is a hallmark of resilient thinking.

Developing healthy coping mechanisms plays a pivotal role in this process. It's about having a toolkit at your disposal that can help you navigate through rough patches. This might include strategies like cognitive reframing, where you learn to challenge and change negative thought patterns, or tactical distraction, allowing yourself short breaks from stressors to enjoy activities that lift your mood and spirit. It's also about setting boundaries and knowing when to say no, preserving your energy for not just the needs of others but for your own.

In cultivating resilience through self-care, you are essentially weaving a safety net that not only catches you when you fall but also helps you climb back up, stronger and wiser. It's about not just surviving the storms but learning to dance in the rain, equipped with your trusty umbrella of resilience. Knowing fully well that the sun also rises, and when it does, you'll be ready to bask in it, rain-soaked lessons in tow.

LEGACY OF SELF-CARE: PASSING ON WELL-BEING PRACTICES

Imagine your self-care routine as a cherished family recipe that's been tweaked and perfected over generations. Just as recipes are passed down, so too can your self-care practices become a legacy, enriching the lives of those around you. Sharing the wisdom of self-care isn't just about telling your friends to try meditation or join a yoga class; it's about integrating these practices into the fabric of your community, making well-being a common goal everyone can strive towards together. When you teach self-care to others, you're not just passing on knowledge; you're fostering a support system where everyone is better equipped to handle life's stressors. It's like teaching someone to fish; you're giving them tools for lifetime resilience and happiness.

Teaching self-care often begins in informal gatherings at home or during heart-to-hearts with friends. It's seen in how you handle stress gracefully and advocate for regular 'me-time,' showing others that it's okay to prioritize their well-being. Encouraging friends to set boundaries or sharing strategies for managing anxiety during coffee meet-ups can ripple through your social circle, inspiring others to take up the mantle of self-care. These moments of sharing become seeds of wellness that, once sown, can grow beyond the individual, potentially transforming a community's approach to health and well-being.

Creating a self-care culture within a community involves championing these practices at every level—from schools and workplaces to local councils and community groups. It's about advocating for policies that recognize the importance of mental health days, pushing for programs offering free yoga classes in community centers, or organizing wellness workshops that address diverse groups' physical and emotional needs. Each initiative, each program, and each policy helps weave self-care into the societal fabric, making it a norm rather than a novelty. This cultural shift can fundamentally alter how communities interact with the concept of health, prioritizing prevention and holistic well-being over mere reaction to illness.

Understanding the ripple effect of your self-care practices illuminates the profound impact they can have on those around you. Each time you choose self-care, you set an example, offering implicit permission for others to do the same. This creates a positive feedback loop in your environment, where self-care becomes a collective priority. The benefits range from reduced healthcare costs to happier, more productive individuals. It's about creating an ecosystem where well-being flourishes, supported by shared knowledge and mutual encouragement.

In essence, your commitment to self-care is not just a personal journey; it's a potential legacy, a gift that keeps on giving. By embedding these practices into your life and sharing them with others, you're contributing to a culture that values and understands the profound impact of caring for oneself. This legacy of well-being is perhaps one of the most significant inheritances you can offer, ensuring that the generations that follow can thrive, not just survive, in the ever-evolving landscape of life.

INTEGRATING SELF-CARE INTO FAMILY LIFE

When it comes to threading self-care into the fabric of family life, think of it as crafting a colorful tapestry that everyone in the family helps to weave. It's about creating a shared artwork where each thread and color represents a unique aspect of care that enriches not just individuals but the family as a whole. This isn't just about scheduling spa days or meditating in silence; it's about integrating practices into your daily routines that nurture everyone's well-being, turning self-care into a communal, joyful endeavor.

Start with the basics: create family self-care rituals that might include anything from Sunday morning yoga sessions to nightly gratitude sharing at dinner. Imagine replacing screen time with green time, where the whole family spends time outdoors, gardening, hiking, or simply playing in the backyard. These activities don't just enhance physical health but also strengthen familial bonds, creating cherished memories. Think about how a simple weekly 'family game night' can serve as a stress reliever, a laughter session, and a lesson in teamwork and resilience all rolled into one. These shared activities are the threads that, over time, become the strong cords holding the family tapestry together.

Modeling self-care for children is perhaps one of the greatest gifts you can give them. Children don't always do what we say, but they certainly see and often emulate what we do. If they see you taking time to read, exercise, or meditate, they're more likely to adopt these habits themselves. Show them that taking care of oneself is not a luxury but a necessity. This can be as simple as involving them in meal preparation and showing them the ins and outs of creating a nutritious and delicious meal. Let them see you managing stress in healthy ways; instead of reaching for your phone at the first sign of stress, maybe do a few stretches or take a few deep breaths. These moments are powerful lessons in self-care, teaching children that their well-being is both important and within their control.

Navigating self-care within romantic relationships often involves a dance of give-and-take. It's about supporting each other's self-care needs while voicing your own. This could look like trading off mornings, where one gets to jog while the other handles breakfast and school prep, then swapping roles the next day. It's about understanding and respecting that your partner's needs might differ. Your idea of self-care is a quiet hour with a book, while theirs might be a loud hour at a spin class. The key here is communication and compromise, ensuring both partners feel supported and valued in their self-care efforts. This mutual respect and support strengthen the relationship and set a profound example for children, showing them that caring for oneself and each other is integral to love and respect.

Balancing individual and family needs often feels like being a circus performer spinning plates on poles, trying to keep them all in the air without letting any crash to the ground. It's a delicate balance, but not impossible. It starts with clearly communicating everyone's needs and strategically planning to meet them without sacrificing your own. It might mean scheduling alone time on the family calendar just as you would any other important appointment. It's about recognizing that your needs don't have to always take a back seat; instead, they can take turns riding shotgun alongside the needs of the family. Maybe it's as simple as taking turns choosing a family activity or setting boundaries around 'me time' where each family member respects others' need for space. This balance is crucial not just for individual health but for the family unit's health, teaching everyone the importance of togetherness and individuality.

In weaving these practices into the fabric of your family life, you create a rich tapestry of care, connection, and mutual respect that not only beautifies your home life but also strengthens each member's ability to face the world outside with resilience, confidence, and a deep-seated knowledge that they are cared for and valued. This is the legacy of self-care within a family—woven with love, strengthened with respect, and cherished across generations.

THE FUTURE OF SELF-CARE: TRENDS AND INNOVATIONS

Imagine you're flipping through a glossy magazine from the future. The pages are splashed with articles about groundbreaking self-care technologies and innovative practices that make today's mindfulness apps look positively quaint. This isn't just fantasy; it's a peek into the trajectory of self-care, where technology and new ideas merge to redefine how we maintain our well-being. The evolution of self-care is an exciting saga of technology meeting human needs, creating solutions that are as smart as they are effective. From apps that nudge you to hydrate or stand up from your desk to virtual reality platforms that can transport you to a tranquil beach for a meditation session, the future is buzzing with potential.

Emerging self-care technologies are already showing us glimpses of this future. Consider wearable devices that track your steps, monitor your stress levels, and suggest activities based on your emotional state. Or think about AI-driven health assistants that can provide personalized diet plans and workout routines, adapting in real-time to your body's feedback. These technologies blend seamlessly into our daily lives, offering tailored self-care interventions that are as unobtrusive as they are personalized. Virtual wellness platforms, for instance, are expanding the boundaries of therapy and coaching, providing access to mental health support that transcends geographical limitations. These platforms use sophisticated algorithms to match individuals with the ideal resources or professionals, ensuring that help is available and appropriate to each person's unique situation.

As these trends evolve, the definition of self-care is expanding. It's no longer just about taking a day off for spa treatments or practicing yoga. It's about integrating intelligent, responsive tools into everyday life to enhance well-being without adding to our to-do lists. Future self-care practices will likely be more preventive than reactive, using data from our daily lives to help avoid stress, burnout, and physical ailments before they start. Imagine a world where your devices remind you to slow down or offer breathing exercises when your heart rate indicates stress. This proactive approach could redefine health care, turning every individual into the best guardian of their own health.

Future-proofing your self-care routine means being adaptable and open to incorporating new practices and technologies as they arise. It involves a willingness to learn and experiment with tools that can enhance your well-being. However, it's also crucial to maintain a core routine that anchors you, regardless of how many new gadgets or apps you try. Balancing innovation with consistency is the key to a self-care routine that is both cutting-edge and deeply nurturing. As you navigate this exciting frontier, blend curiosity with caution, embracing new tools that enhance your well-being while holding fast to the timeless practices that support your health. This balance will ensure that your self-care routine remains robust, responsive, and equipped to meet the challenges of tomorrow.

SUSTAINING A SELF-CARE MINDSET AND PRACTICES BEYOND 30 DAYS

Think of your self-care as your favorite Netflix series; you wouldn't want it to end after just one season, right? The goal is to renew it season after season, with each one bringing new insights, challenges, and growth. The 30-day self-care journey is merely the pilot episode. Once you've tasted the transformative effects, the trick is to keep the momentum going and build upon it, making self-care a continuous and evolving script in the sitcom of your life.

Transitioning from a 30-day journey to a lifelong commitment might sound daunting, like deciding to run a marathon after your first 5K. But it's about shifting perspectives. It's not a sprint; it's more like a scenic route that you decide to explore deeper every day. The end of the 30 days is not the finale; the cliffhanger leaves you wanting more.

This phase is about integrating self-care into your daily fabric, making it as habitual as your morning coffee. It's about recognizing that self-care isn't a luxury or a temporary fix; it's as crucial as breathing.

Committing long-term to self-care means embedding it into your ethos, not just your schedule. It's about cultivating a mindset where self-care is perceived as necessary as eating or sleeping. This commitment might mean saying no to late nights at work to protect your sleep schedule or prioritizing your budget for health and wellness just as you would for other essentials. It's about setting non-negotiables—at least 30 minutes a day on activities that nourish you, whether reading, walking, or simply doing nothing. And yes, doing nothing can be a profound act of self-care, too!

To sustain these self-care practices, keep exploring, adjusting, and embedding these habits into the very core of your daily living. Let each day be an opportunity to refine, enhance, and deepen your commitment to well-being. Remember, self-care is not a destination but a way of traveling through life. With each step, you are not just moving forward but evolving, adapting, and thriving.

Reflection Section: Self-Care Toolkit

"Self-care is a conscious choice to uplift yourself with people, places, experiences, and opportunities that recharge your personal battery and promote holistic wellbeing – body, mind and spirit."

NONIE ADAMS, STRENGTHS AND RESILIENCE
COACH

Envision your perfect self-care toolkit. What essentials would you include today (acknowledging that this may well change in the future)? For a truly balanced life, ensure your toolkit contains at least one or two resources tailored to each facet of your self-care regime. Take a moment with your journal to ponder and reflect.

Then, begin to assemble your ultimate self-care toolkit using descriptions, imagery, or any creative expression that resonates with you.

CONCLUSION

As we draw the curtains on this enlightening journey of self-care, let's take a moment to reflect on the rich tapestry we've woven together. From the fascinating intricacies of neuroplasticity to the soothing simplicity of mindful breathing, we've traversed a landscape that's as diverse as it is deep. As we've discovered, this journey isn't about reaching a lofty destination but about embracing the winding path of holistic well-being that connects our lives' physical, emotional, mental, and social fibers.

Throughout this book, we've unpacked the neuroscience that underpins our habits, explored bite-sized, actionable strategies that fit neatly into our busy lives, and delved into the reflective practice of journaling to deepen our self-understanding. We've also embraced a growth mindset and cultivated resilience, tools that support our self-care routines and empower us to face life's unpredictable waves with grace and grit.

What sets this guide apart isn't just its commitment to cutting-edge research or its customizable approach to self-care; it's how these elements come alive in an engaging format that speaks directly to you—yes, you with the tea in one hand and dreams in the other. This book was designed not just to inform but to transform; not just to be read but to be experienced.

Remember, the art of self-care is deeply personal. What works for one may not work for another, and that's perfectly okay. This book is your starting block, not your finish line. Use it as a springboard to dive deeper into your needs, experiment, and discover what makes you feel vibrant and alive.

And let's not forget the power of our community. Share your stories, your struggles, and your victories. Engage with others on this path because the strength we need can sometimes be found in the stories we share. Self-care is not just a personal journey; it's a communal voyage that thrives on mutual support and understanding.

 So, as you move forward, remember this: Prioritizing your well-being isn't a luxury—it's essential. It's not selfish; you must be your best self, for yourself, and for those you love. You are worth every minute you invest in your health and happiness.

Thank you for walking this path with me. May your self-care journey be as rewarding as it is enlightening. Here's to flourishing in every sense of the word—today, tomorrow, and beyond. Remember, the best time to plant a tree was twenty years ago. The second-best time is now. So, go ahead, plant your self-care tree, and watch it grow!

MASTER SELF-CARE FOR WISE WOMEN

An Empowering 30-Day to Enhance Holistic Well-Being, Deepen Self-Reflection and Find Your Pathway to Inner Peace

Now that you have everything you need to master self-care, it's time to pass on your newfound knowledge and show other readers where they can find the same help.

By leaving your honest opinion of this book on Amazon, you'll help other wise women find the information they're seeking and inspire them to embrace self-care.

Thank you for your help. Sharing our knowledge keeps the importance of self-care for women alive, and you're helping women to do just that.

How to Leave Your Review

Simply scan the QR code below to leave your review:

REFERENCES

Rousseau, D. (2023, December 5). Neuroplasticity–Rewiring your brain through mindfulness. Retrieved from https://sites.bu.edu/daniellerousseau/2023/12/05/neuroplasticity-rewiring-your-brain-through-mindfulness/

Medical News Today. (n.d.). Cortisol and stress: The relationship explained. Retrieved from https://www.medicalnewstoday.com/articles/cortisol-and-stress

Graybiel, A. M., & Grafton, S. T. (2019). Dopaminergic mechanisms in actions and habits. _Frontiers in Psychology, 10_. https://www.ncbi.nlm.nih.gov/pmc/articles/PMC6673057/

Meyer-Lindenberg, A. (2016). Oxytocin and social functioning. _Nature Reviews Neuroscience, 17_(7), 440-452. https://www.ncbi.nlm.nih.gov/pmc/articles/PMC5573563/

Mind Tools. (n.d.). What are your values? - Deciding what's important in life. Retrieved from https://www.mindtools.com/a5eygum/what-are-your-values

Scott, E. (2021, September 20). 11 SMART goals examples for life improvement. Retrieved from https://www.lifehack.org/864427/examples-of-personal-smart-goals

Southern New Hampshire University. (n.d.). Why is self-care important? Retrieved from https://www.snhu.edu/about-us/newsroom/health/what-is-self-care

Forbes Coaches Council. (2022, October 26). An effective time management strategy for ambitious and busy women. Retrieved from https://www.forbes.com/sites/forbescoachescouncil/2022/10/26/an-effective-time-management-strategy-for-ambitious-and-busy-women/

Mayo Clinic. (2023, January 1). Depression and anxiety: Exercise eases symptoms. Retrieved from https://www.mayoclinic.org/diseases-conditions/depression/in-depth/depression-and-exercise/art-20046495

Gunnars, K. (2023, April 15). 17 proven tips to sleep better at night. Retrieved from https://www.healthline.com/nutrition/17-tips-to-sleep-better

Harvard Health Publishing. (2023, June 7). Mindful eating: A review of how the stress-digestion connection affects the gut-brain axis. _Harvard Health Blog_. https://www.ncbi.nlm.nih.gov/pmc/articles/PMC7219460/

Medical News Today. (2019, July 12). Can 'forest bathing' reduce stress levels? Retrieved from https://www.medicalnewstoday.com/articles/325060

Council for Relationships. (n.d.). Benefits of mindfulness on women's health.

Retrieved from https://councilforrelationships.org/benefits-of-mindfulness-on-womens-health/

Harvard Health Publishing. (2018, June 15). Six relaxation techniques to reduce stress. Retrieved from https://www.health.harvard.edu/mind-and-mood/six-relaxation-techniques-to-reduce-stress

Abhasa Rehabilitation and Wellness Home. (2022). The impact of diet on women's mental health. Retrieved from https://abhasa.in/articles/impact-of-diet-on-womens-mental-health/

Jafari, E., & Ghanbari, F. (2021). Effects of positive psychology interventions on happiness in women with unintended pregnancy: A randomized controlled trial. _Heliyon, 7_(10). https://www.sciencedirect.com/science/article/pii/S2405844021018922

American Psychological Association. (2023, June). The science of why friendships keep us healthy. _Monitor on Psychology_. Retrieved from https://www.apa.org/monitor/2023/06/cover-story-science-friendship

Gil, N. (2022, September 11). How to communicate better with your friends, advice from a therapist. _CNBC_. Retrieved from https://www.cnbc.com/2022/09/11/how-to-communicate-better-with-friends-advice-from-a-therapist.html

Noonday Collection. (2023, February 22). The importance of community for personal growth and well-being. Retrieved from https://blog.noondaycollection.com/the-importance-of-community-for-personal-growth-and-well-being/

HelpGuide. (2023, April 5). Setting healthy boundaries in relationships. Retrieved from https://www.helpguide.org/articles/relationships-communication/setting-healthy-boundaries-in-relationships.htm

Diversus Health. (2022, October 3). The mental health benefits of creativity. Retrieved from https://diversushealth.org/mental-health-blog/the-mental-health-benefits-of-creativity/

Harvard Health Publishing. (2018). Spirituality and well-being: Theory, science, and the practice of holistic health. Retrieved from https://www.ncbi.nlm.nih.gov/pmc/articles/PMC8651234/

Mindful Staff. (2014). Getting started with mindfulness. _Mindful_. Retrieved from https://www.mindful.org/meditation/mindfulness-getting-started/

UC Davis. (2023, May 15). Why does experiencing 'flow' feel so good? _UC Davis Curiosity Blog_. Retrieved from https://www.ucdavis.edu/curiosity/blog/research-shows-people-who-have-flow-regular-part-their-lives-are-happier-and-less-likely-focus

Burns, J., & O'Connor, D. (2018). The neuroscience of goals and behavior change. _Frontiers in Psychology, 9_. https://www.ncbi.nlm.nih.gov/pmc/articles/PMC5854216/

Columbia University Irving Medical Center. (2022, March 10). What to do about self-care fatigue. _CUIMC Newsroom_. Retrieved from https://www.cuimc.columbia.edu/news/what-do-about-self-care-fatigue-conversation-lourival-baptista-neto-md

The Good Trade. (2023, January 1). 99 inexpensive self-care ideas for your new year. Retrieved from https://www.thegoodtrade.com/features/self-care-ideas/

Yau, L. (2023, January 12). 8 ways to cope with life transitions. _Psychology Today_. Retrieved from https://www.psychologytoday.com/us/blog/the-addiction-connection/202312/8-ways-to-cope-with-life-transitions

Massage Mastery Online. (2023). Embracing growth: Carol Dweck's growth mindset and its application in adult education. Retrieved from https://massagemastery.online/embracing-growth-carol-dwecks-growth-mindset-and-its-application-in-adult-education/

Nourish App. (2023, February 28). 5 powerful emotional resilience practices for women. Retrieved from https://www.thenourishapp.com/post/5-powerful-emotional-resilience-practices

Woombie. (2023, March 5). 4 ways to incorporate self-care into your family's routine. Retrieved from https://woombie.com/blog/post/4-ways-to-incorporate-self-care-into-your-familys-routine

McKinsey & Company. (2023, December 30). The top wellness trends in 2024. Retrieved from https://www.mckinsey.com/industries/consumer-packaged-goods/our-insights/the-trends-defining-the-1-point-8-trillion-dollar-global-wellness-market-in-2024

ABOUT THE AUTHOR

Amazon.com: Nonie Adams: books, biography, latest update

Made in United States
Orlando, FL
24 September 2024

51906214R00083